stupid
SOCK CREATURES

s t u p i d
SOCK CREATURES

**Making Quirky,
Lovable Figures
from Cast-off
Socks**

John Murphy

LARK BOOKS

A Division of Sterling Publishing Co., Inc.
New York

Library of Congress Cataloging-in-Publication Data

Murphy, John (John C.), 1975-
  Stupid sock creatures : making quirky, lovable figures from
cast-off socks / by John Murphy.
      p. cm.
  Includes index.
  ISBN 1-57990-610-9 (pbk.)
  1. Textile crafts. 2. Socks.   I. Title.
TT699.M85 2005
745.592'4--dc22

                                                    2004022762

10 9 8 7 6 5 4 3 2 1

Published by Lark Books, A Division of
Sterling Publishing Co., Inc.
387 Park Avenue South, New York, N.Y. 10016

© 2005, Text and illustrations, John Murphy
© 2005, Photography, Lark Books

Distributed in Canada by Sterling Publishing,
c/o Canadian Manda Group, 165 Dufferin Street
Toronto, Ontario, Canada M6K 3H6

Distributed in the United Kingdom by GMC Distribution Services,
Castle Place, 166 High Street, Lewes, East Sussex, England BN7 1XU

Distributed in Australia by Capricorn Link (Australia) Pty Ltd.,
P.O. Box 704, Windsor, NSW 2756 Australia

The written instructions, photographs, designs, patterns, and
projects in this volume are intended for the personal use of the
reader and may be reproduced for that purpose only. Any other
use, especially commercial use, is forbidden under law without
written permission of the copyright holder.

Every effort has been made to ensure that all the information in
this book is accurate. However, due to differing conditions, tools,
and individual skills, the publisher cannot be responsible for any
injuries, losses, and other damages that may result from the use
of the information in this book.

If you have questions or comments about this book, please contact:

Lark Books
67 Broadway
Asheville, NC 28801
(828) 253-0467

Manufactured in China

ISBN 13: 978-1-57990-610-8 (paperback)
        978-1-57990-966-6 (kit paperback)
ISBN 10: 1-57990-610-9 (paperback)
        1-57990-966-3 (kit paperback)

For information about custom editions, special sales, premium
and corporate purchases, please contact Sterling Special Sales
Department at 800-805-5489 or specialsales@sterlingpub.com.

Editor: Joanne O'Sullivan

Art Director: Dana Irwin

Cover Designer: Barbara Zaretsky

Photographer: www.keithwright.com

Assistant Art Director: Lance Wille

Associate Art Director: Shannon Yokeley

Editorial Assistance: Delores Gosnell

Dedication

For Ms. Carl Clark who saw the creatures' potential. And for West Oakland's own Dominic Payne, whose potential I see.

contents

Introduction

Forgive me if I stare at your ankles. Forgive me if I hand you a business card and ask you to give me your socks when you're done with them. I've been sculpting with socks for almost two years and they've become a bit of an obsession with me. A sock isn't good or bad based on its quality or comfort, but whether or not it'll make a good monster.

I've come to be known to some as "the Stupid Creatures guy." I love to sculpt and I love monsters. The Stupid Creatures phenomenon started when I tried my darnedest to make a sock monkey, but wound up making my first creature, Albertine. A little while before, I'd given up my ceramics studio in Berkeley, California to save money to move back home to North Carolina. The sculpting itch didn't go away, so without clay, I turned to a heaping trash bag of worn-out socks I'd been collecting.

After Albertine came a slew of other delightfully strange little beasties. Is it a cat? Is it a bunny? Maybe it's both, but it's probably neither. People liked my "stupid creatures"—a name that stuck and became official. My odd little babies—swarming all over the world, wreaking cute havoc. I'm the proudest parent ever.

This book offered me the unexpected opportunity to bring the stupid creatures home to you (and with any luck help me pay off my student loans). What you have here is a smattering of techniques that span the entire Stupid Creatures repertoire of design. The book has three sections. First we'll go over the technical instructions that apply to all the patterns in this book, and any creature you might make on your own after learning from the book.

The eight patterns in the next section cover every trick and technique I employ in making the creatures. Once you've got a handle on the basics, you can do Syd-like ears on a Jordan-esque body. You can put a bone through Genevieve's head and create your own, one-of-a-kind creature. You might even develop new techniques, unique to you, and have a monster above and beyond anyone's expectations. Next comes the gallery section, which features pictures of other creatures I've done, including some great shots of creatures with their new owners.

I chose the eight patterns so that there'd be some harder ones, like Genevieve and Claude, and some easier ones, like Owlsley and Red Wetty. But when I had my patterns established, I noticed a really intriguing visual chemistry among them.

I hope you'll be able to start tinkering with leftover scrap material and matchless socks you have lying around and make something out of nothing. Trash to treasure, as they say. Take what you learn in this book and expand upon it. Create something fantastic and enjoy it. Let others enjoy it as well.

SUCH DRIPPY SMARM!

ZEN AND THE ART OF

YOU CAN
SEE IT.

IF YOU
WANT...

I made
the first stupid creatures out of
my old socks, but customers also
send me their castoffs. I'm sure that if
you scrounge through your drawers,
you'll find odd socks, matchless
ones, or a pair or two you can
part with for a creature.

CREATURE-MAKING

Stuff You'll Need

* Socks

Chances are, since you're likely to be using old socks, you're bound by circumstance and won't really put much thought into the socks you wind up using. I encourage you to be, I guess, "Zen," about the choice of material you use, but do consider the vastly different types of socks and the effects you can expect to get from them.

Stretchy socks take more stuffing to fill them and tend to become a tad sheer the fuller they become. The darker your stretchy socks are, the more stuffing you'll see through them at certain angles. It'd be nice if polyester fiberfill came toned, but as far as I know, you're limited to white. Because stretchy socks hold a lot of stuffing, you can plan on having a large creature. Cotton and nylon socks (novelty ones with pictures and things) are incredibly stretchy. I personally prefer natural fibers over synthetic ones because they are a bit less sheer when stuffed to capacity.

* Tip: Socks to Use *

All of the instructions for this book involve the use of crew socks, which have a distinctive heel and extend to the mid-shin/mid-calf. If you can get socks with heels and toes in different colors, great. It isn't necessary though. You can "transplant" a different-colored heel onto a solid-colored sock such as a tube sock (see page 33). Ankle socks, bobby socks, or any sock with little or no tube won't be suitable for these projects, but that isn't to say that such socks are useless for creature-making. You just have to transplant tubes from other socks and remove or extend the cuffs of the short ones. Knee socks are also useful, just count on a longer, larger creature, or plan to cut off excess material.

Have you ever been on the road behind a bunch of competitive cyclists all decked out in their stretchy gear? Every now and again you can spot evident wear on one of their backsides. When the cyclist selects the riding pants before donning them, the fibers aren't stretched, so he or she might not realize the fabric is wearing thin. But as soon as he or she is on the bike and in motion, the worn areas become almost as revealing as a pair of pantyhose. You can still perceive the color of the material, but undergarments or nature's blessings are clearly seen through. I'm reminded of this effect whenever I've stuffed a stretchy sock too fully. To avoid this type of result, stuff your creature lightly.

Big, knobby, knitted socks made from really thick yarn are probably going to unravel as soon as you cut into them. Thick wool socks have the least amount of stretch and make really sturdy creatures.

Sometimes argyle socks or ones with woven patterns can be turned inside out for a nifty effect. Consider this technique for fuzzy, hairy-looking creatures.

✳ BUTTONS AND EYES

Eyes for your creature are a matter of taste. I use old buttons primarily, in keeping with the whole recycling/reuse philosophy. For the first hundred or so creatures I used a particular kind of button that was white with a dark blue circle in the center. These buttons looked so much like cartoon eyes that for a while I couldn't fathom using anything else. When my supply of these buttons (which were bought at a junk shop and therefore had no manufacturing information) started to run low, I really freaked out. I found a reasonably similar substitute and used those until they ran out. Eventually I just resorted to using buttons of any size and shape.

Big, knobby, knitted socks made from really thick yarn are probably going to unravel as soon as you cut into them.

I tend to use matching buttons for a pair of eyes, or the same button in two different sizes. It's important to me that the eyes match, or at least complement one another. In cases of three eyes, I think all three buttons should match perfectly, otherwise any two that are alike will be the only ones that register as eyes, especially if there's a third button in between them that's slightly different. This button might register as a nose. Any number of buttons above three might start looking less like an array of eyes and more like an array of buttons. Two of them might stand out as the official eyes in your own mind.

HEY COME BACK HERE! YOU DON'T HAVE ANY EYES YET!!

Sometimes I'll combine two buttons to make one eye, putting a smaller button on top of a larger one and stitching them in place together. The results are really neat, especially if the larger button has a dent that can carry the smaller one flush inside. With different color and texture combinations, you'll have a better chance at customizing the eyes to the particular creature you're making.

Refer to the diagram below for the terms I use for parts of a sock. The TOE is where your toes

Parts is Parts

go, the INSTEP is the part that surrounds your foot. The HEEL is where your heel goes (as if you didn't know). The TUBE is what I'm calling the upper part of the sock where the opening is, and which surrounds your ankle and leg when the sock is pulled on. Some people call it the CUFF or the RIBBING. Those terms, I think, apply to specific features that not all socks share, which is why I'm foregoing them in favor of the word "tube."

A layman's anatomy of a sock

TOE
INSTEP
HEEL
TUBE
CUFF

✳ OTHER STUFF

Some sharp fabric scissors. Fabric scissors are recommended over craft or paper scissors. They cut smoothly and effortlessly through all fabrics thick and thin without fraying or snagging the fabric. They're a bit of an investment, but they make all the difference when making small cuts, as we will surely do throughout this process.

Sturdy needles. Stay away from quilting, embroidery, or milliner's needles—they're too tiny. For stitching the mouths, use 4- to 5-inch (10.2 to 12.7 cm) long doll needles. For sewing the stuff-hole shut and putting on button eyes try sturdy 2-inch (5 cm) long needles.

Pins with glass heads. I like these because they're longer and sturdier than their counterparts. They're also much more visible and less likely to be left inside a creature by mistake.

A point turner. This is a flat, smooth piece of plastic that's pointed at one end and blunt at the other. It's used when you turn a sewn item right side out and want to get the corners as turned out as possible.

HELLO, MY NAME IS

LARZ

Sometimes corners are tough because of the way the fabric bunches in them and you can't just stick your finger in and make them pop out all the way.

Thread. Use 100 percent polyester thread for the majority of your sewing (polyester-cotton blends can fray or snap) and upholstery thread for sewing the mouths and closing the creature's stuff-holes. It's super strong and can take a lot of pulling and tugging without breaking or fraying. It's also incredibly smooth and slides through multiple layers of fabric quite easily.

Polyester fiberfill or cotton stuffing. I like polyester fiberfill because these days you can often buy it recycled.

Seam ripper. If you're using a sewing machine, you'll surely need one of these from time to time.

Thimbles. You'll need some, unless you want to develop calluses on your fingertips.

A sewing machine. You can hand-stitch these monsters, too. It just takes a bit longer.

Scrap fabric or little add-on items as you need or want them. Among my favorites are tulle, ribbon, jingle bells, and other thingies.

Tip: Measuring

Don't. All of these patterns were created by eyeballing and guessing. It's best if you do that with your socks, since all socks are different. The measurements shown in the diagram are proportional to the sock shown and you would be wise to follow such proportions based on the size and shape of your socks. Measurements given are estimates. If you can't make cuts in exactly the same dimensions or proportions shown in the diagrams, make your cuts proportionally sound to the size of your sock.

Cutting

Most of the diagrams will involve arranging your sock heel-side up with the toe at the top. Sometimes for the sake of clarity, a diagram will depict a sock on its side. The toe will still be at the top. Some cuts need to be made with the sock on its side, and diagrams for those instances will be provided. It's likely that those diagrams will show what your sock should look like after prior cuts have been made and pieces of material removed.

Seam allowance: Necessary, but plan it.

Seam allowance reduces stuffable space. Remember that whatever you sew usually needs to be turned right side out again and stuffed. Don't get caught with too little room.

The Cut	Stitching with seam allowance	The result

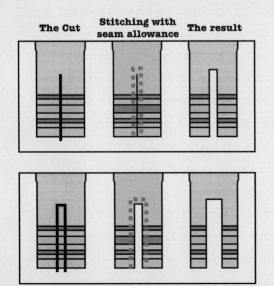

* This measurement is based on a ¼-inch (6 mm) seam allowance

Sewing

Seam allowance is the space between the stitching and the raw edge of the fabric. Seam allowance is incredibly important because of how some socks tend to fray or roll when cut. All seam allowances in this book are ¼ inch (6 mm). Sometimes, according to the nature of your sock fabric, you might have to increase your seam allowance (if it's really stretchy, or tends to roll up, or frays easily), or you might be okay decreasing it.

When deciding where and how long to make your cuts, always bear in mind that wherever there's a raw edge, you'll lose ¼ inch (6 mm) of width from the sewing. For example, if you're cutting legs from a sock's tube, only make one vertical cut. When you stitch those raw edges, you'll have a ¼-inch (6 mm) seam allowance on either side of the cut, which will separate the legs by ¹/₂ inch (1.3 cm) or so. There is seldom any need to cut fabric away from in between the legs, unless you're going for a particular effect like Estelle's incredibly wide gait (see page 64).

Anytime you see the word "stitch," it means to backstitch by hand (see fig. 1a), unless specified otherwise. If that stitch doesn't work for you, you can find other alternatives below. If you're using a sewing machine, which I do, use a straight stitch, setting your width to 0 and your length to 2.

Since this book caters to hand-sewers, it doesn't necessarily account for the following eventualities, but if you wind up with too little seam allowance because of a mistaken cut, or if your edge is frayed

where you want to sew, use a zigzag stitch on your sewing machine. Set the width to 4 or 5, and the length to 0.5 or 1, and sew close to the edge so that the outer swing of the stitch falls on the outside of the raw edge. This makes a very secure seam and eliminates fraying. If you're sewing by hand, use the overcast stitch (fig. 1c), keeping the stitches very close together.

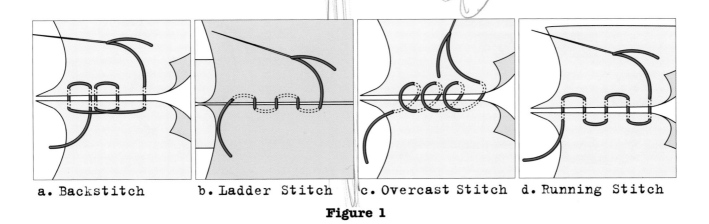

a. Backstitch   b. Ladder Stitch   c. Overcast Stitch   d. Running Stitch

Figure 1

Pinning

You should pin corners that touch or wherever you plan to place a seam. You should also pin wherever stripes and other solid color changes occur.

Pin stripes (or anywhere there's a color change like from toe to instep) to hold the point of color transition in place while you're stitching so it'll match up when you turn the item right side out.

Proper pinning goes down through both layers of fabric, then back up through both layers, with probably no more than $1/8$ inch (3 mm) between entry and exit points. The wider apart your entry and exit points are, the more likely it is that the layers of fabric will be out of alignment when your pin exits.

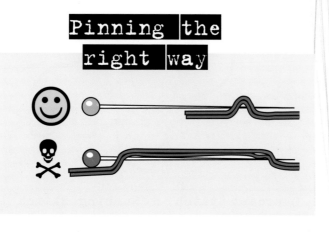

Pinning the right way

Knotting

If you're hand sewing, knot the end of your thread or make six to nine small, tight loops before making your first stitch. Use the French knot method (fig. 2) to secure your stitch when you've finished a seam.

If you're machine-sewing, start by straight stitching about $1/8$ inch (3 mm), reverse stitch over it, and stitch forward to the end of your seam. Then reverse stitch $1/8$ inch (3 mm) again, and forward to the end of your seam.

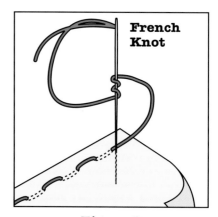

French Knot

Figure 2

Stuffing

Use polyester fiberfill. It's incredibly soft and uniform, lacking any lumps or knots. You might even be able to find recycled ("grade 2") polyester fiberfill.

Stuff gradually. Use small pieces bit by bit. Avoid cramming large fistfuls of stuffing into your creature. First off, you'll never hope to delicately fill a narrow limb or a tapering tail or tentacle all the way to the tip if you cram.

Cramming also causes nonuniform lumps and hard nodules, which look disquieting and tacky.

If you're stuffing an entire body at once, one that, perhaps, has horns or long ears at the top, start with small bits of stuffing and stuff the long extremities first, working your way into the head and down the neck. Stop and stuff any arms the creature might have. Continue stuffing the creature down through the torso, then finish with the legs (fig. 3).

Wherever your fingers can't reach, use the closed tip of your scissors, a $1/4$-inch (6 mm) wooden dowel, or something called a "stuffing tool." I don't think you'll need one of those. Just like you don't really need a fish fork, a salad fork, or a cake fork.

STUFF! DON'T CRAM!

This is the basic sequence by which you should stuff your creature. It's probably obvious to most of you that you start from the farthest point away from the opening and work your way back, but I'll explain it just to be on the safe side.

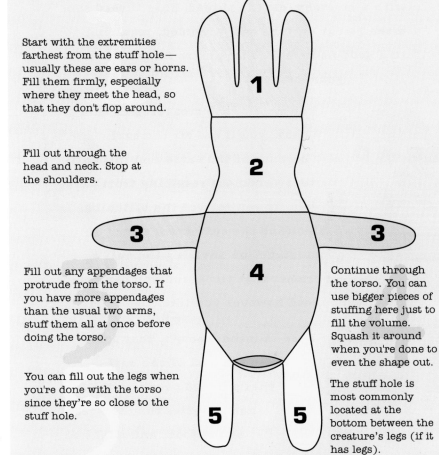

Start with the extremities farthest from the stuff hole— usually these are ears or horns. Fill them firmly, especially where they meet the head, so that they don't flop around.

Fill out through the head and neck. Stop at the shoulders.

Fill out any appendages that protrude from the torso. If you have more appendages than the usual two arms, stuff them all at once before doing the torso.

You can fill out the legs when you're done with the torso since they're so close to the stuff hole.

Continue through the torso. You can use bigger pieces of stuffing here just to fill the volume. Squash it around when you're done to even the shape out.

The stuff hole is most commonly located at the bottom between the creature's legs (if it has legs).

SEMANTIC ISSUE: Stuffing something "firmly" means stuffing it evenly in a way that fills out the shape, stretches all the creases without compromising the seam, and props the body up so that it needs no interior support to keep from flopping.

TIP: Prevent runs in your stuff hole by zigzag or overcast stitching its perimeter before you stuff.

Figure 3

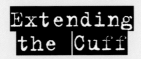

Tip:

Extending the Cuff

Some sock cuffs (if you look on the inside of the sock) are folded over and stitched down with a stretchy, elastic thread. This thread can often be cut and the cuff unfolded, resulting in a good ½ inch (1.3 cm) extra length of your material.

For most of the creatures in this book, you'll cut off the cuff because of the extra and inconsistent thickness resulting from that fold. If you release the stitching, holding the cuff down, any instruction advising the cuff's removal is moot, and you can proceed however you like.

Bear in mind, though, that sometimes the part of the cuff that's folded over is a thinner material than the rest of the sock, and might be useless for your project, in which case you'll need to trim it off anyway. You be the judge of that.

Attaching the Limbs and Appendages

Limb attachment can be done a number of ways, and the same process can be applied to any tubular appendage you may wish to add. Yes, you can think nasty thoughts. It makes no difference to me, but don't go telling the judge I taught you how to make your creatures gender specific. I'll explain how to do it in three methods: the circumference method (page 23), the slit method (page 24), and ladder stitching (page 25). Genevieve (page 88) is the only exception, as her four arms were attached with an overcast stitch (see page 19, fig. 1c) to the outside of her body after it was stuffed.

The creatures you see in this book have had their limbs attached, where applicable, using the circumference method. I prefer it to the slit method, which allows limbs to flop around. The ladder-stitching method might be easier for some of you than the other two methods, but I think it looks like body-part transplant sutures, like you might have seen on Dr. Frankenstein's monster had Mary Shelley been more descriptive. There's nothing wrong with ladder stitching—I just don't care for the effect.

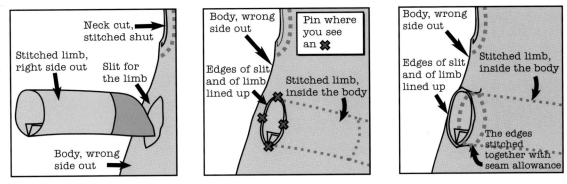

Figure 4

✳ THE CIRCUMFERENCE METHOD

Once the limb you intend to attach is sewn, don't stuff it. Keep it right side out. The body to which you intend to attach the limb should be wrong side out. Insert the limb into the body, closed-end first, aligning the seam with the point of the slit you've cut for the limbs attachment. The edge of the open end of the limb should line up with the edge of the seam. Secure the limb to the slit with two to four evenly placed pins. Backstitch along the circumference of the two aligned edges, leaving at least a $\frac{1}{4}$-inch (6 mm) seam allowance. When you've stitched the entire circumference, turn out the limb so that it is now wrong side out, and on the outside of your creature's body. The circumference method works quite well for horns and tails as well as for limbs (see fig. 4).

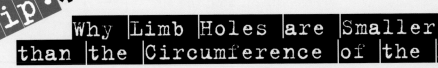

✳Tip:✳ Why Limb Holes are Smaller than the Circumference of the Limb

Material is stretchy. I make the limb holes small then stretch the hole out to a more suitable size for the limb. This makes it possible to put more limb holes in or around the same area of the monster, for example, attaching multiple horns to the head. Sometimes the holes you're making for the arms come precariously close to the side cuts for the neck. Making a smaller limb hole and stretching it is far easier than trying to arrange and work with precariously close holes. There's also the matter of seam allowance. You want at least $\frac{5}{8}$ inch (1.6 cm) between each hole, because each one is going to use a $\frac{1}{4}$-inch (6 mm) seam allowance, and you don't want to cause problems with overlapping.

Tip:

Combining Different Material

If you use different socks, I strongly suggest you make sure they're the same fabric or are similar in weight and stretchiness. If your socks are substantially different, like stiff wool to stretchy nylon, whichever parts of your sewn-together creature are stretchier will wind up larger in proportion to the stiffer material when you stuff them (they'll look swollen). There will also be uneven strain on the stretchier fabric at the stitching points. This might result in seams popping or runs forming over time. If you're one of those conceptual artists to whom such disquieting incongruity appeals, then combine as you will.

* THE SLIT METHOD

Make sure the body is turned wrong side out, and that your stitched limb is turned right side out and stuffed already, having left a good $1/4$ inch (6 mm) of empty space at the end.

Insert the limb, seam down and closed end first, into the limb slit on the body (see fig. 5a).

Line the open edge of the limb with the edge of the slit.

Pinch the lined-up edges of the slit and the limb together, and pin all layers of fabric together to hold them in place (see fig. 5b).

Stitch all four layers together, closing off both the slit and the limb opening (see fig. 5c).

Turn the body right side out. Knot your thread, and turn the body inside out. The finished limb should hang freely from the body, with all evidence of attachment concealed within.

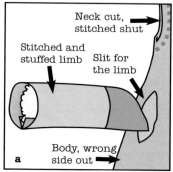

Neck cut, stitched shut
Stitched and stuffed limb
Slit for the limb
a Body, wrong side out

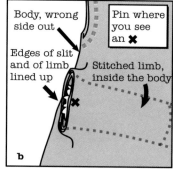

Body, wrong side out
Pin where you see an **✗**
Edges of slit and of limb lined up
Stitched limb, inside the body
b

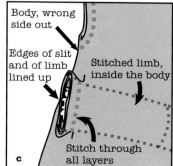

Body, wrong side out
Edges of slit and of limb lined up
Stitched limb, inside the body
Stitch through all layers
c

Figure 5

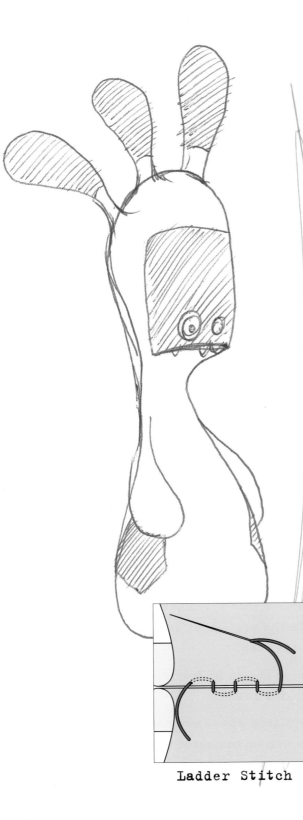

✷ LADDER STITCHING

Once the raw edges of your limbs are sewn, turn the limb right side out and stuff it. Pick the spot on your already-stuffed body where you think the limb should go. Ladder stitch (see below) the limb to the body, making the stitches as small as possible, perhaps two-or-three-fibers-of-sock-material wide so you don't get that Boris Karloff sutured look, unless you want it.

Ladder Stitch

✷Tip:✷

No Science to Any of This

Making a sock monster the **Stupid Creatures way is all about discovering new tricks and ways to manipulate the material. If while following any of these instructions you get inspired to follow your own muse, DO IT. Your monster will be that much more unique and beautiful (or horrible...the good kind of horrible).**

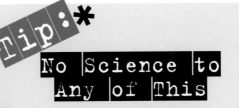

Sewing the Mouths (fig. 7)

This is a fun part. I seriously love this part because you'll start to notice your monster's personality as the mouth forms. I like to start smack in the middle of the heel and work my way first to one side, back to the middle, out to the other side, and back to the middle again.

Firmly anchor the end of your thread about ¹/₄ to ¹/₂ inch (6 mm to 1.3 cm) in from one of the corners of the heel.

Imagine a horizontal divide connecting the corners of the heel (I call it the "equator" of the heel). Enter the heel with the needle at the equator, just a tiny bit away from the anchoring point.

Exit at the top edge of the heel. Re-enter the heel at the top edge, about ¹/₈ to ¹/₄ inch (3 to 6 mm) further towards the middle of the heel from where you just exited. Scoop your needle downward to gather as much stuffing as you can. This action fills out the lips. You'll need to do this all the way across the mouth.

Exit the heel after this downward scooping motion, about ¹/₈ inch (3 mm) above the imaginary divide. Re-enter the heel about ¹/₈ inch (3 mm) below the divide.

Visual Aids

The cutting and stitching lines on the illustrations are approximations of where to work your material. Measurements are given only as needed, and even then aren't set in stone.

* The cutting lines are solid, and the stitching lines are dashed, though sometimes a thinner dashed line will be used to show something under or inside something else.

* When you see a faded object, it indicates that the portion is being cut away. Often you'll save this spare part for another step in the project, or another project down the road.

* Shapes shown in gray are wrong side out.

* The places where you need to pin will be indicated with a squat X.

Scoop downward to collect stuffing, and exit the heel at its edge directly below your original anchor.

Re-enter the heel about $^{1}/_{8}$ to $^{1}/_{4}$ inch (3 to 6 mm) further towards the middle of the heel. Remember to exit below and re-enter above the equator. When you exit at the top edge of the heel, exit at or close to the re-entry point of the previous loop. Keeping these loops close together reduces lumpy lip syndrome and keeps the pair of lips smooth.

About halfway through the process, you'll start to notice the heel becoming a pair of lips. They might be thin or wide. It doesn't matter at all.

You can stitch widely ($^{1}/_{4}$ to $^{5}/_{8}$ inches [6 to 1.6 mm] apart) working from the center just to establish the lips. When you reach the edge, or wherever you want to stop, repeat this technique going back toward the center with narrower stitches ($^{1}/_{16}$ to $^{1}/_{8}$ inch [1.6 to 3 mm] apart) to reduce lumpiness and even out the lips.

✳ LIP LUMPS

As you form the mouth, you'll notice peaks where there are no stitches, and valleys where the stitches are. To eliminate these peaks, create stitches that are about $^{1}/_{8}$ to $^{1}/_{16}$ inch (1.6 to 3 mm) apart to reduce the size of the peaks. As soon as your peaks are small enough, stitch over the tops of the peaks (spearing your needle from valley to valley) to force them down, kind of like cinching up a belt to hold your belly in.

Repeat this all the way back to the center. Do it again on the other side.

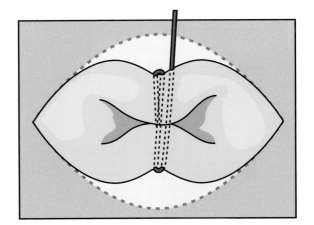

Figure 7

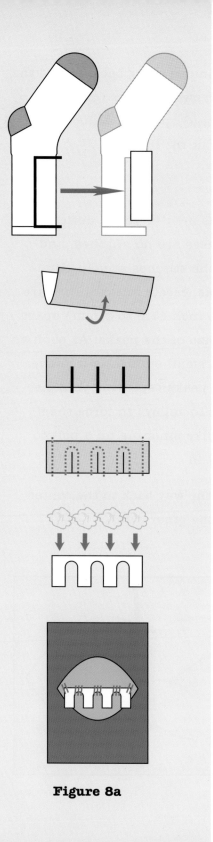

Figure 8a

✳ MAKING BUCK TEETH (FIG. 8a)

Cut 1/2 x 3/4-inch (1.3 x 1.9 cm) rectangles out of your favorite tooth-colored fabric (anything light and pale works well for this). Use triangles for fangs, and make them about 1/2 inch (1.3 cm) longer. Arrange them right side touching right side. Stitch the raw edges together from the fold to the opening. As a finished tooth remains basically inert with no pressure or stress from play, this sort of feature requires less seam allowance than a limb or a horn. Leave maybe 1/8 inch (3 mm) for seam allowance. Turn the tooth inside out (it will look like a teeny tiny bag), stuff it lightly, and attach it with a few overcast stitches to the "equator" of the heel.

✳ CREATING TONGUES (FIG. 8b)

Cut a 2 x 1-inch (5 x 2.5 cm) rectangle of your favorite tongue-looking fabric.

Fold the strip short end to short end, with the wrong side out.

Stitch the raw edges together in a rounded or tapering U-formation. The curve of the U should be at the fold of the strip. Trim the corners off the curve of your tongue, and turn it right side out.

Lightly stuff the tongue. Make it plump but not huge. Don't pack it or round it out. You want it to stay basically flat.

Take the stuffed tongue and stitch a straight line from the open end to within $3/16$ inch (5 mm) from the tip. This makes a reasonably convincing tongue-ish crease.

✳ ATTACHING TEETH AND TONGUES

Once you've created a set of teeth or fangs or a tongue, establish the horizontal middle of your creature's mouth, and stitch the open ends of the oral features there. Then, just follow the lip-stitching instructions (see page 27) as normal. You'll really love how a mouth with features turns out.

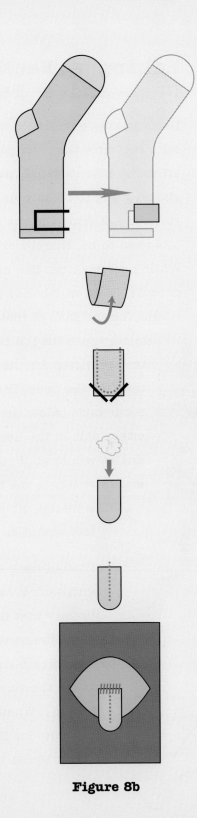

Figure 8b

Making a Neck, or a Neck and a Tail

Neck making consists of making four vertical cuts below the intended mouth of your creature. Like gastric bypass surgery, you're going to be snipping off bits of material and stitching the cut shut where those bits used to be, thereby creating a crimp. While neck making, like any step in this process, has a number of possible variations, for the sake of instruction, we will assume you want the heel for the mouth, the toe/instep for the head, and the tube for the body. The four cuts will occur once below the heel, once on either side of the heel (like where the ankles would go if you wore the sock), and once where the tube blends into the instep, where the top of the foot would go (fig. 9a).

Though neck sizes will vary with each creature design, let's just say that the cuts for the chin and the back of the neck will be 1 inch (2.5 cm) long, and the cuts for the sides will be $^1/_2$ inch (1.3 cm). When you make the four cuts for the neck, be careful not to cut very deep since you always need to account for seam allowance. Seam allowance will more greatly reduce the stuffable space of your creature's neck. If you're doing the tail variation of these instructions, the back neck/tail cut will be essentially 3 to 4 inches (7.6 to 25.4 cm) long, or as long as you need it to be. You'll end this cut where you think your creature's butt will be (fig. 9b).

Be especially careful on the sides of the neck. Don't cut too deeply in or make your cuts too long, as you might interfere with where the arms are placed, if your creature's getting arms. Sometimes your side neck cuts only need to be a slit, rather than a curved cut like the chin and the back. You be the judge. For the sake of visibility, this diagram will feature curved cuts on all sides of the neck.

I like to make the chin cut a bit more pronounced than the others. I make it a deep curve, or almost an upside down L.

Here's how you do it:

Make all your cuts. It doesn't matter right now if the sock is wrong or right side out.

Turn the sock wrong side out, if it isn't already. Vertically stitch shut the cuts you made for the front, back, and sides of the neck (fig. 9c and 9d).

Seam allowance is very important here because of the stress put on the neck when stuffing. It's often a tight squeeze for all the stuffing going into the head and you don't want to pop a seam. Leave a good ¼-inch (1.3 cm) seam allowance.

If you cut your slits too deeply and can't leave enough seam allowance, close your cuts with a closely stitched overcast, or, for you machine users, use a zigzag stitch with a width of 4 and a length of 0.5 to 1.

Once you've made your stitches, turn the sock right side out again and look at your work (fig. 9e and 9f). You should notice a definite crimp in the width of the sock. This'll remain a very convincing neck when you stuff your creature. And because of the reduced amount of space, the stuffing within the neck will be firm enough to support the head. It looks so great in real life.

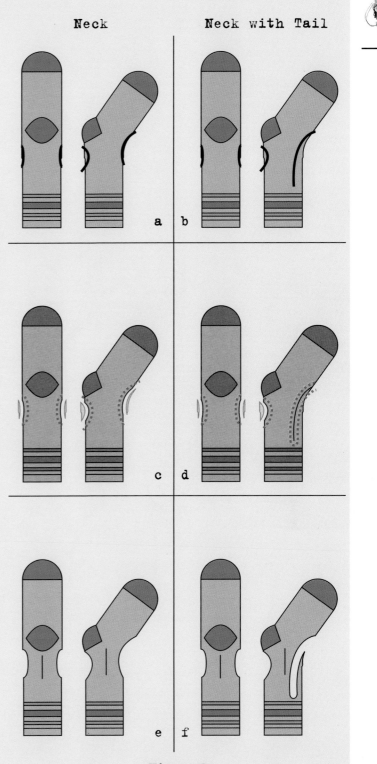

Neck   Neck with Tail

a b

c d

e f

Figure 9

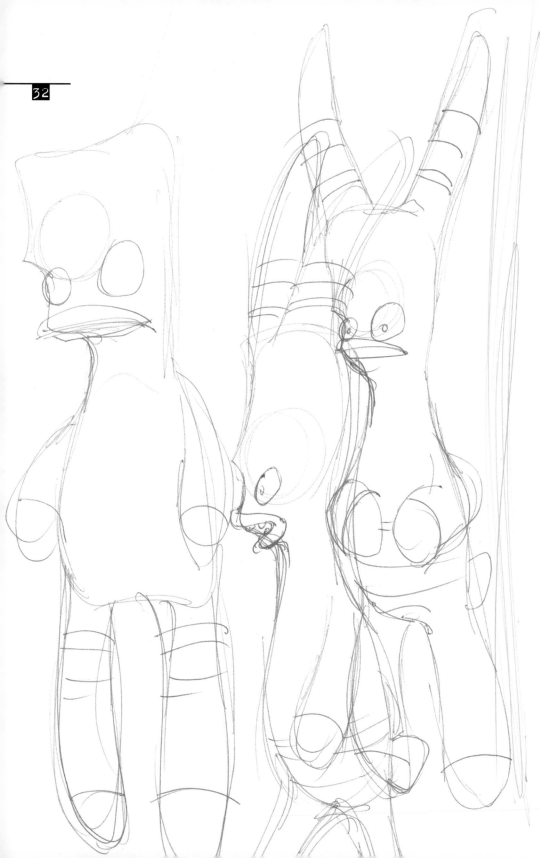

Whether or not you want to do a neck is entirely up to you. You don't have to, but I find that adding a neck gives the creature a bit of distinction and helps to separate the head from the rest of the body. Necks vary. Sometimes you won't have enough room on your creature for side cuts because you need a place for the arms. That's totally fine. Some creatures, like Red Wetty (see page 52) and Syd (see page 72) don't have necks at all.

✱ STITCHING THE NECK CUTS SHUT

This is really easy. Just stitch in a lengthwise manner, leaving a 1/4-inch (6 mm) seam allowance. If you're making a tail from the back neck cut, just stitch the whole cut closed in a U-formation starting from the top of the neck and ending at the tip of the tail.

Tip:

Putting a Heel of a Different Color on a Solid-Colored Sock

If the heel of your sock is worn out, or if you want your creature's mouth to stand out more, you can transplant a heel from a different colored sock, bearing in mind the difference in material, onto the one you want to use for your creature. Here's how you do it:

Turn your donor sock to the side, matching up the corners of the heel and the seam in the toe. Smooth out all wrinkles. Snip out the heel like you're cutting a wedge of cheese or slice of pizza (see fig. 6a).

Turn your transplant recipient sock to the side, matching up the corners of the heel and the seam of the toe. Smooth out all wrinkles. Remove a wedge of the heel that's slightly smaller than the heel you're transplanting. Turn this sock wrong side out (see fig. 6b).

Pin the corners of the donor heel, wrong side out, to the corners of the hole you've just cut in your recipient sock, right side touching right side. Also pin the top and the bottom edges of heel and hole together, right side also touching right side. Stitch the two layers together along both edges using the circumference method leaving a ¼-inch (6 mm) seam allowance (see fig. 6c). You can also overcast if you want.

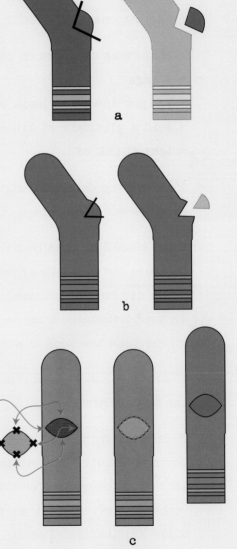

Figure 6

Toe Socks

You see them on hippies and ladies with big chunks of amethyst. You want to set them on fire. They're obnoxious, and, frankly, quite uncomfortable. But they exist and we must deal with them. These are suggestions for how to use our friends, the toe socks.

- **Mohawks or chicken combs**
- **Wings**
- **Ridges down the back or sides**
- **And a plethora of other things you might think of...**

Here are the detailed instructions for how to make wings out of toe socks.

Now, since I'm usually making an entire creature out of a pair of toe socks, I normally use only about one-third of the sock, or, proportionally, a segment just a bit longer than the sock is wide.

✖ Arrange your obnoxious toe sock with the toes pointing up.

✖ Starting from the big toe side, make a horizontal cut about half the width of the sock. Cut downward vertically about $1/2$ inch (1.3 cm) longer than the cut you just made. Go horizontal again, cutting through to the pinky toe side of the sock.

✖ Turn the severed toe part wrong side out.

✖ Backstitch (see page 19) shut the first horizontal cut (from the big toe side) and the vertical cut.

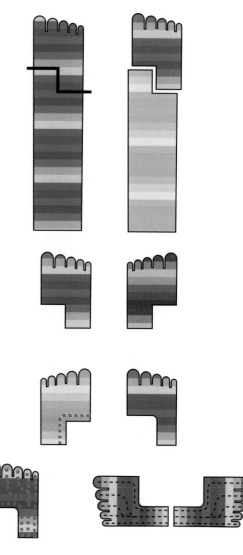

Figure 11

- ✖ Leave the other horizontal cut open.

- ✖ Turn the wing right side out.

- ✖ Stuff the wing lightly. If you have quilt batting, use just one layer. You don't want this shape rounded out, but you do want to give it a little substance. If you had to quantify the thickness, I'd suggest a $^1/_4$ inch (6 mm).

- ✖ The quilter in you will love this part. Once your wing is stuffed, you have to anchor the stuffing in place by quilting the wing. You can do this with any pattern you choose. Try stitching in kind of a bat wing pattern. It looks really neat.

There you go. You've made a wing. Attach it onto the back of your creature with the slit method (see page 24).

For all other applications of the infamous protuberances of the toe sock, just cut the toes off with no less than $^1/_2$ inch (1.3 cm) of instep, and attach it to the head, back, sides, or wherever else you want on your creature via the slit or circumference methods (see pages 24 and 25). If you want to use the slit method, cut off 1 inch (2.5 cm) or more of the instep with the toes so you'll have some room for adequate stitching and stuff it before you attach it. For an example of toe socks in action, see the Mighty Klimzon (page 102), Slzappa (page 103), and Gruphudd Eubanks (page 105).

Caring for Your Creature

The best way to care for your creature is to handle it gently, as if it were a puppy or a kitty—one that you didn't want to kill. These sock monsters, can handle a little roughhousing from time to time, though.

When it's time to clean your creature, wash it carefully by hand in cold water with detergent suitable for hand-washed dainty underthings. Or you can machine wash it on the gentle cycle with similar colors. Polyester fiberfill is machine washable, and so are socks. The only thing you have to worry about is possibly repositioning/redistributing the stuffing within your creature once it's dry again.

Line dry or tumble dry your creature on low heat.

If only a spot on the creature is dirty, try to get it out with a damp cloth and a little dainty-underthings liquid.

I'M SO IN LOVE WITH YOU.

THE CREATURES

This book is about sharing the techniques I've discovered just by messing around. These creature instructions are approximations based on their proportion to the size and shape of the sock you use. There are no exact measurements. The only concession I'll make along those lines is that to make creatures similar in proportion to the ones I've made, you should use the same kind of socks used for the instructions. If your socks are longer or shorter, you can cut them down or add extra material.

The techniques used for these creatures will
serve as springboards to newer and more
complicated methods that you'll discover for
yourself. It was kind of accidental that I
even started making the stupid
creatures, so I'd like you
to discover some happy
accidents for yourself
as you create.

JORDAN

Jordan is confident that you will utterly screw up his pattern. In fact, he's slept very little over the course of the week anticipating all your prospective blunders. If you decide to make this pattern, do it without his knowing.

> WHY SHOULD I EVEN BOTHER INTRODUCING THIS PATTERN. I'LL ONLY BE IGNORED AGAIN.
>
> I SHOULD HAVE TAKEN THAT DOOR-TO-DOOR DENTISTRY JOB.

You Will Need

2 socks, identical if possible

Buttons for eyes

Scissors

Sewing machine or needle and thread

Instructions

Cutting the Parts for Jordan

Place both socks with the heel facing up and the toe at the top. Cut one sock from the middle of the toe to about one-third of the way between where the toe ends and the heel begins. Then, coming in from the sides, make 45° cuts that connect with your first cut. Do this from both sides (fig. 1a).

From the cuff of that sock, snip the corners off at around a 60° angle (fig. 1b).

You're going to dismember the second sock into lots of little pieces. Make sure your scissors are nice and sharp! Make a horizontal cut about 1 inch (2.5 cm) or so above the heel, severing the toe from the instep. You'll get the legs from this piece (fig. 1c).

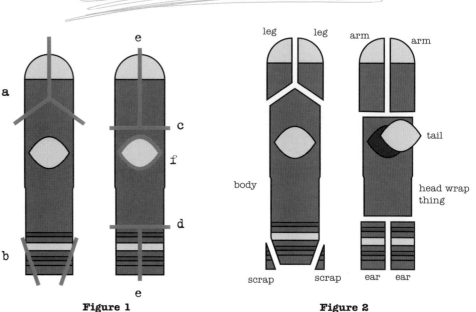

Figure 1

Figure 2

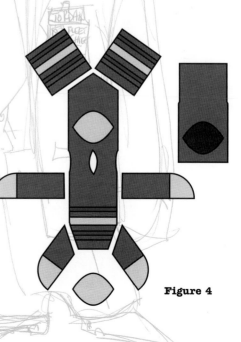

Make another horizontal cut that severs about half of the tube from the rest of the sock. This piece will become the ears (fig. 1d).

Cut the severed toe segment and the severed tube segment in half lengthwise (fig. 1e).

Carefully cut out the heel from the remaining segment. The heel will become the tail (fig. 1f).

What remains from this sock will be used for Jordan's headdress. You can make one if you want or you can use this piece of sock for another creature (fig. 2).

Go back to the first sock, the one you removed the toe bits from. This sock is the body of your Jordan creature. Turn this sock to the side, lining up your previous cuts and the corners of the heel.

Make the neck cuts according to the instructions on page 30 (fig. 3a).

No less than ¹/₂ inch (1.3 cm) below the cuts you made for the sides of the neck, cut a ¹/₂-inch (1.3 cm) vertical slit for the arms. Make sure to cut through both layers of the sock (fig. 3b).

Parts Overview (fig. 4)

All of your pieces should now be cut for your Jordan creature. You should have:

a badly disfigured majority of 1 sock for the head and body

2 short toe bits for the legs

2 long toe bits for the arms

2 tube halves for the ears

1 disembodied tail and a heel-less midsection of 1 sock for the headdress

Figure 3

Figure 4

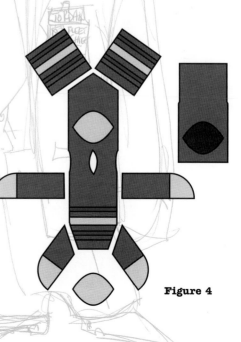

Stitching Jordan Together

STITCHING THE EARS

First, turn the body sock inside out. Stitch shut the cuts you've made for the neck according to the instructions on page 30. Lay the body flat, heel side up, with the cuff of the body at the bottom.

Grab one of the squares of tube you made for the ears. Arrange it right side up like this (fig. 5a).

Figure 5a

Fold the top edge down to meet the bottom edge (fig. 5b).

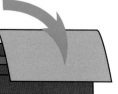

Figure 5b

Pin the edges together near the corners and stitch from edge to fold leaving a ¼-inch (6 mm) seam allowance (fig. 5c).

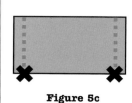

Figure 5c

Turn the ear so that the newly made seams face you (fig. 5d).

Figure 5d

Pin the seams together at the edges where they meet, and stitch from a side fold, just over the seam, and then immediately down to the open edge (fig. 5e).

Figure 5e

Then turn it right side out and BING, you have an ear. Repeat these instructions with the other ear (fig. 5f).

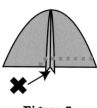

Figure 5f

Stitching the Ears to the Head

Grab the body sock, keeping it right side out. You remember that peak leftover where the toe bits were removed? It's now the top of the head (fig. 6a).

Place a pin at the top corners of both layers of material. Make a stitch across the head opening, leaving one-quarter of the opening on either edge unstitched and open (fig. 6b).

Now that those instructions for the ear are all taken care of, you have a little ear. It might look to you kind of like a baby's bootie. Whatever it looks like to you, orient it so that the opening is up (fig. 6b).

You've made your stitch at the top of the head, which left you with two openings for the ears to slip down into. Insert the ear into either of these holes. Match up the seam of the ear with the point where the head seam ends (fig. 6c).

Pin those seam points together, and stitch the ear edge to the head opening edge using the circumference method (see page 23).

Repeat these instructions for the other ear.

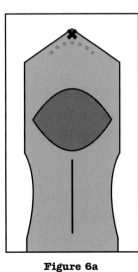

Figure 6a

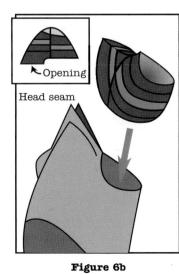

Opening

Head seam

Figure 6b

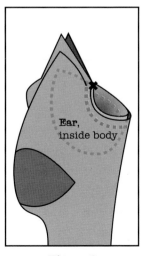

Ear, inside body

Figure 6c

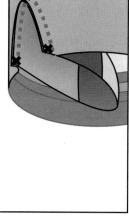

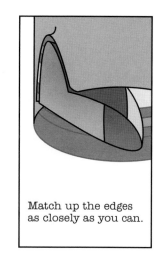

Body sock wrong side out.

Slit, with edges turned out slightly

Toe bit

Figure 7a

Match up the edges as closely as you can.

Figure 7b

Figure 7c

STITCHING THE LEGS

So, now you've got a toe bit and the body sock with the neck and tail sewn.

Arrange the toe bit beneath one of the slits in the cuff of the body sock. The edge of the toe bit ought to match up with the size of the slit, but it really

doesn't matter unless the toe bit's edge is much bigger than the slit. In this instance, cut the slit a little deeper in the body sock to compensate (fig. 7a).

Arrange the edge of the toe bit inside the slit of the body sock with right sides touching (fig. 7b).

The vertex of the slit should match up with the edge of the toe bit at its fold. The corners of the slit and the toe bit should correspond.

Pin the two pieces together at the corresponding corners and at the meeting of the toe bit's fold and the slit's vertex (fig. 7c).

Stitch the two edges together. Remember the seam allowance of at least $1/4$ inch (6 mm). Turn the toe bit out so that it hangs from the outside of the body.

Repeat these steps with the remaining toe bits. Once you've done one, the rest should be a snap.

STITCHING THE ARMS

Grab the two toe bits you've set aside for the arms. Turn them wrong side out, and stitch them shut from the toe to the instep (fig. 8).

Stitch the arms to the body using either the circumference method (see page 23) or the slit method (see page 24).

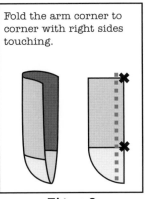

Fold the arm corner to corner with right sides touching.

Figure 8

STITCHING THE TAIL

Arrange the disembodied heel right-side up, with the corners at the top and bottom (fig. 9a)

Fold it corner to corner with the right sides touching (fig. 9b).

Stitch from the fold down towards the corner (fig. 9c).

When you get within $^3/_8$ to $^1/_2$ inch (9.5 mm to 1.3 cm) from the corner, change direction and stitch straight out to the edge (fig. 9c).

Turn the tail right side out and trim the corners (fig. 9d).

Attach it to the body via the slit or circumference methods or by ladder stitching (see pages 23, 24, and 25 respectively).

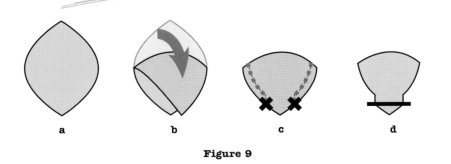

a   b   c   d

Figure 9

PUTTING ON THE HEADDRESS

You probably notice that there isn't really a diagram for Jordan's headdress, except the one depicting its existence. All you really do to achieve head-dressedness for Jordan is slip the piece of un-heeled instep over Jordan's head so that his ears pop out the top of it and his face shows through the heel hole. Roll down the head-dress from the top. **Muy facil.**

CONGRATULATIONS! Your Jordan is assembled! Go ahead and gently turn him right side out, and stuff and finish him according to the instructions on page 21.

OWLSLEY

This is one of the easier patterns, but if you say that to Owlsley himself, make sure his face is buried in a book so he won't notice the implication that he, himself, is simple. 'Cause he isn't. He's quite smart, but easily offended.

IT MIGHT BE BEST IF I JUST DID THIS PATTERN FOR YOU. YOU CAN HAND ME PINS.

You Will Need

1 pair of socks, matching if possible

About 6 inches (15 cm) of the thin part of a necktie

Buttons for eyes

Scissors

Needle and thread or sewing machine

Cutting the Parts for Owlsley

Arrange your socks so that they're both heel up with the toe at the top (fig.1).

On one sock, cut a 45° V-shape between the heel and the toe. This will be the upper face/forehead of your creature (fig. 2a). Save the severed toe for another monster.

From the cuff of this sock, make a vertical cut up the middle of the tube. Make the cut around 3- to 4-inches (7.6 to 10.2 cm) long, or about half the length of the tube, or however long you want. This cut will separate the legs (fig. 2b).

For the next steps on this sock's torture agenda, follow the neck-making instructions found on page 30 (fig. 2c).

Figure 1

a

b   **Figure 2**

c

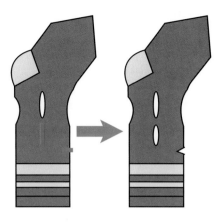

Figure 3

Next, make ¹/₂-inch (1.3 cm) arm slits anywhere between the side neck cuts and the end of the leg cut. Make a horizontal ¹/₂-inch (1.3 cm) slit about ³/₄ inch (1.9 cm) above the end of the leg cut. This will be the slit for the tail (fig. 3).

Move on to the next sock. Cut it vertically from the middle of the toe to about halfway between where the toe ends and the heel begins (fig. 4a).

Coming in from the sides, make 45° cuts that connect with your first cut. Do this from both sides. These pieces will become the arms (fig. 4b).

Next, remove a vertical half of the tube. This will be the tail (fig. 4c).

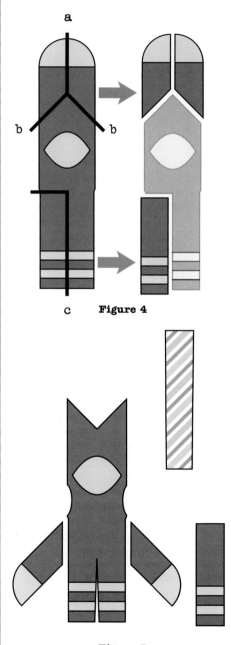

Figure 4

Figure 5

Parts Overview (fig. 5)

At this point you should have:

The body

Necktie segment

2 toe bits for arms

Half of a tube for the tail

Stitching Owlsley Together

STITCHING THE HEAD

First and foremost, turn all the cut body pieces wrong side out. Stitch the cuts you made for the neck according to the neck-making instructions on page 30.

Fold the strip of necktie fabric in half horizontally with the right side out (fig. 6a).

Insert the folded necktie strip into the top of the head, folded end first. Leave enough necktie visible to clear the angles of the top of the head. Place pins at the corners of the cut at the top of the head, securing the necktie segment in the middle of the head. Stitch along the raw edges of the head cut, straight across the necktie, leaving a 1/4-inch (6 mm) seam allowance (fig. 6b).

STITCHING THE LEGS

Let's travel down to the cuff of the sock. This part is easy.

Place pins at the edges of all the stripes, if you have stripes.

Stitch along the edge of the cuff, turning up at the vertical cut that separates the two legs. Stop within 1/2 inch (1.3 cm) of the top of that cut (fig. 7).

Do this again on the other leg.

STITCHING THE ARMS

Grab one of the toe pieces you've cut for the arms. Turn it wrong side out, and place pins at the corners and at the

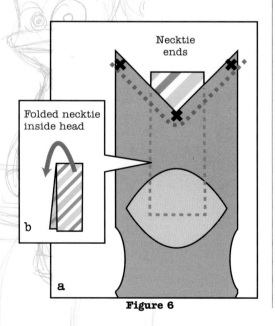

Necktie ends

Folded necktie inside head

b

a

Figure 6

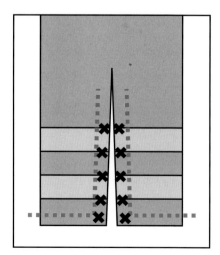

Figure 7

end of the toe where the color changes into the instep. Stitch straight from the point of the toe straight up to the corner (fig 8).

Repeat these instructions for the other arm.

Turn the arms right side out, and attach them to the arm slits in the sides of the body via the circumference method (see page 23).

STITCHING THE TAIL

Take the segment of tube you cut for the tail and turn it wrong side out. Place pins at the corners and at the edges

of all the stripes, if you have stripes. Stitch along the cuff from the fold towards the raw edge. Turn the piece and stitch along the entire raw edge (fig. 9)

Turn this tail right side out and attach it to the tail slit on the back of the body using the circumference method (see page 23).

Finish Owlsley's mouth according to the instructions on pages 26, then sew on his eyes. You can hang him on your car's antenna by the necktie loop in his head.

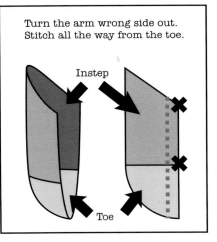

Turn the arm wrong side out.
Stitch all the way from the toe.

Instep

Toe

Figure 8

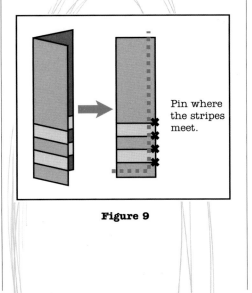

Pin where the stripes meet.

Figure 9

RED WETTY

Red Wetty might look wide-eyed and simple, but he's no village idiot. Do a good job on his pattern and you'll win his grumbling respect for years and years. Do a bad job, and he'll probably just ignore you. But doing no job at all will put you on Red Wetty's bad side for the rest of your life. You might wake one day to discover that your home's water main has been rerouted through your sewage line, so don't skip over this pattern just 'cause Red Wetty's short.

You Will Need

2 mismatched socks, similar in material weight, and stretchiness

$1/2$ x 1-inch (1.3 x 2.5 cm) rectangles, at least 4 for the teeth of white/tooth colored scrap sock material

Buttons for eyes

Scissors

Needle and thread or sewing machine

Cutting the Parts for Red Wetty

Decide which of your two different socks you want for the body.

Make cuts above and below the heel according to fig. 1. Make sure you leave plenty of room between the heel and both of the cuts for eyes and seam allowance once the creature is stitched.

Next, turn your body sock segment to the side and flatten it so that your cuts and the corners of the heel line up. Make a vertical cut about ¹⁄₂-inch (1.3 cm) long, slightly below and at least ¹⁄₂ inch (1.3 cm) beyond the corner of the heel (fig. 2). Make sure you cut through both layers of the sock. Then, from the edge opposite the heel, make a horizontal cut about ¹⁄₄ inch (6 mm) into the body, no less than 1 inch (2.5 cm) above the bottom of the body segment (fig. 2). This is where the tail will be sewn in.

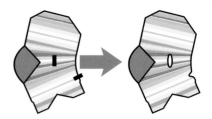

Figure 2

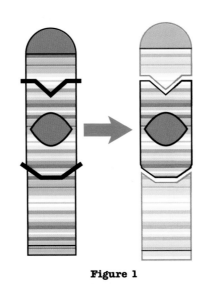

Figure 1

Cut the tube off your second sock (fig. 3a) then cut the cuff off the tube (fig. 3b).

Cut the tube in half horizontally, then cut one of the tube halves into equal quarters. These will be the arms and legs. Cut a curved tail from the other half of the tube as shown in the fig. 3c.

Parts Overview (fig. 4)

At this point you should have:

1 body sock
2 bits for arms
2 bits for legs
1 tail bit
1 rectangle for the teeth

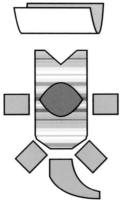

Figure 4

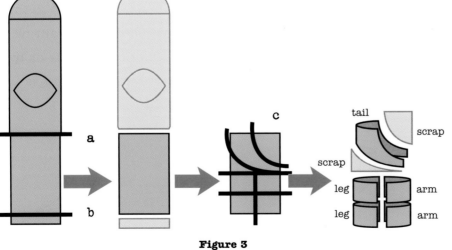

Figure 3

Stitching Red Wetty Together

STITCHING THE TEETH

Follow the instructions for making buck teeth on page 28. Make as many or as few teeth as you want or as will fit.

STITCHING THE ARMS

Fold the arm rectangles (which are identical to the leg rectangles) in half horizontally with the right sides touching (fig. 5a).

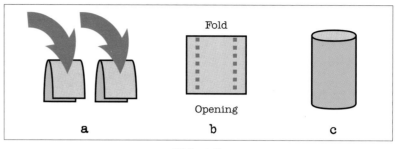

Fold

Opening

a   b   c

Figure 5

Stitch both edges from the fold to the corners leaving as much seam allowance as you can, preferably $1/4$ inch (6 mm) (fig. 5b).

Turn the limbs right side out (fig. 5c).

You can attach these to the body using either the slit or circumference methods or by ladder stitching (see pages 23, 24, or 25 respectively).

STITCHING THE TAIL

Fold the tail shape in half with the right sides touching (fig. 6a).

Stitch the raw edges as shown in fig. 6b. You'll stitch along the fold. Don't let this bother you. It's really no big deal.

Trim the corners of the seam allowance at the tip of the tail.

Turn the tail right side out. Use the tip of your scissors or a point turner to get the tip turned out as best you can (fig. 6c).

You can attach the tail to the body using either the slit or circumference methods or by ladder stitching (see pages 23, 24, or 25 respectively).

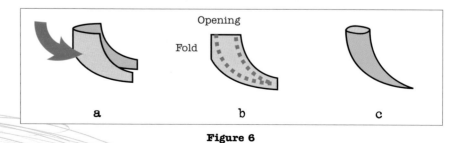

Opening

Fold

a   b   c

Figure 6

STITCHING THE LEGS TO THE BODY

Turn the body wrong side out. Notice the bottom of it. The opening is diagonal on both sides. These diagonals are where the legs will be attached. The horizontal middle part of the body's opening will be left open for stuffing.

Pin the short edges of the legs to the diagonals of the opening. If the legs and the diagonals aren't the same length, gently stretch whichever one is smaller. Don't worry about this. The whole thing's gonna stretch all over the place when you stuff it (fig. 7a).

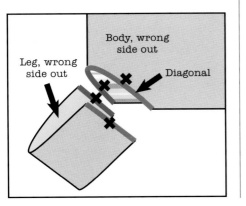

Figure 7a

Once the leg is attached to the body, pin the attachment points together seam to seam. Stitch shut the raw edges of the leg as shown (fig. 7b). It's okay to overstitch a little into the body. This makes a smoother looking transition from leg to body.

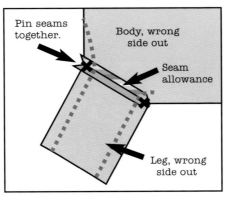

Figure 7b

STITCHING THE EARS AND THE TOP OF THE HEAD

Nothing could be easier and more straightforward. Just stitch shut the raw edges leaving a $^1/_4$-inch (6 mm) seam allowance (fig. 8).

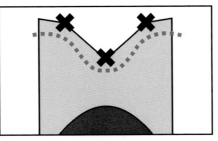

Figure 8

Finishing Red Wetty

You're done stitching. Now turn the little horror right side out and stuff him firmly, but not so firmly that you cause runs.

Stitch the stuff hole shut with a ladder stitch (see page 25) or a stuff-hole stitch.

Follow the instructions for attaching teeth (see page 27), then finish the lips as indicated on page 28.

W R O N K Y

Wronky will likely be too distracted by his surroundings to care whether you put an ear where a leg or an arm should be, but to ensure his basic functionality, try your best to follow these instructions.

"AU GRATIN." THAT WORD JUST REALLY STICKS WITH ME. "AU GRATIN."

AND TO THINK IT MEANS "COVERED IN CHEESE." THAT'S JUST FASCINATING!

You Will Need

2 socks, identical if possible, but definitely similar in substance

Buttons for eyes

Scissors

Needle and thread or sewing machine

Cutting the Parts for Wronky

Place both socks with the heel facing up and the toe at the top.

Cut one sock from the middle of the toe to about one-third of the way between where the toe ends and the heel begins. Then, coming in from each side, make a 45° (or thereabouts) cut that connects with your first cut. The resulting toe pieces will be Wronky's arms (fig. 1).

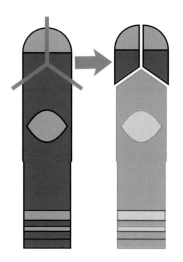

Figure 1

This first sock will be Wronky's head and body. Follow the neck-making instructions on page 30 to make the neck. Then, no less than $1/2$-inch (1.3 cm) below the side neck cuts, make $3/4$-inch (1.9 cm) vertical slits for the arm holes (fig. 2).

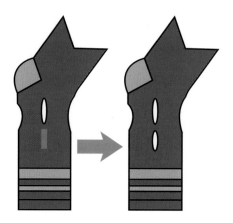

Figure 2

You're going to hack the second sock into all kinds of fun pieces. Everybody sharpen your lawnmower blades.

Make a horizontal cut about 1 inch (2.5 cm) above the heel severing the toe from the instep (fig. 3a).

Cut this toe segment in half vertically to separate the legs (fig. 3b).

Remove most of the tube with a swift, swashbuckling horizontal cut (fig. 3c).

Cut the severed tube in half vertically. These pieces will be the ears (fig. 3d).

Fig. 3e only exists to illustrate the separated halves of ear tube. You can ignore it if you want.

Parts Overview (fig. 4)

All of your pieces should now be cut for your Wronky creature. You should have:

1 seriously mutilated big piece of sock for the head and body

2 short toe bits for the arms

2 long toe bits for the legs

2 tube halves for the ears

1 disembodied heel for the tail

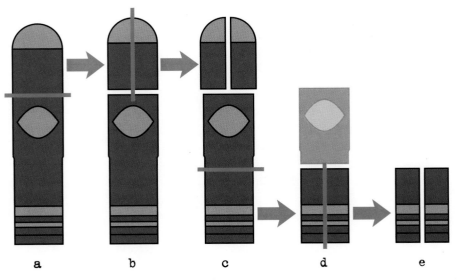

Figure 4

a   b   c   d   e

Figure 3

Stitching Wronky Together

STITCHING THE LEGS

Let's do the legs first since they're weird. Once you've done the legs, the ears are easy.

Keep the legs right side out. We're not stitching them shut yet.

Insert the legs, toe first, into the cuff of the body (fig. 5).

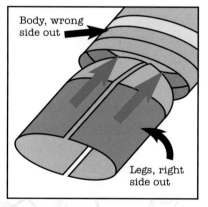

Body, wrong side out

Legs, right side out

Figure 5

Line up the edges of the legs with the cuff of the body. Pin the layers together at the corners of the legs' edges and at the legs' folds. Stitch around the edges, leaving a ¼-inch (6 mm) seam allowance (fig. 6).

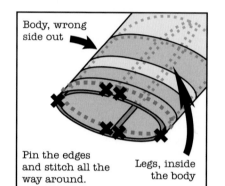

Body, wrong side out

Pin the edges and stitch all the way around.

Legs, inside the body

Figure 6

Pull the legs out so that they're wrong side out like the rest of the body.

Stitch from the toe to within ½ inch (1.3 cm) of the top of the legs. You don't want to sew the legs shut entirely 'cause you need a stuff hole (fig. 7).

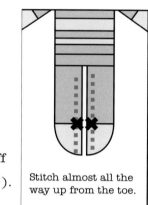

Stitch almost all the way up from the toe.

Figure 7

STITCHING THE NECK

Stitch the neck cuts shut according to the neck-making instructions on page 30.

STITCHING THE EARS

The ears are done in a manner almost identical to the legs. Keep them right side out, and insert them all the way into the head (fig. 8).

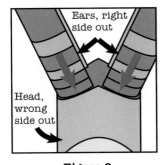

Figure 8

Line up the edges of the ears with the diagonal cuts of the head. Pin the layers together at the corners of the ears' edges and at the ears' folds (fig. 9).

Stitch around the edges, leaving a 1/4-inch (6 mm) seam allowance (fig. 9).

Pull the ears out so that they're wrong side out like the rest of the body. Pin the ears at the stripes and the top corners at the seams you just made at the top of the head (fig. 10).

Pick an ear and stitch from the corner at the fold in a curve that ends up at the raw edges of the ear where it's attached to the head. Continue stitching across the top of the head, and up the other ear the same way you stitched the first one. Remember to leave a seam allowance (fig. 10).

Trim any excess material, especially at the tips of the ears, but don't trim too close to the seam allowance.

STITCHING THE ARMS

Turn the arms wrong side out. Stitch the open edges from the toe straight upward (fig. 11).

Turn the arm right side out, and attach it to the body via the slit or circumference methods or by ladder stitching (see pages 23, 24, and 25, respectively).

Finishing Wronky

Turn the little bugger right side out.

Stuff your Wronky creature as firmly as you want according to the stuffing instructions on page 21.

Stitch shut the stuff hole using a ladder stitch or an overcast stitch (see page 19).

Stitch the mouth according to the mouth-making instructions on page 26.

Sew on buttons for eyes wherever you think they should go.

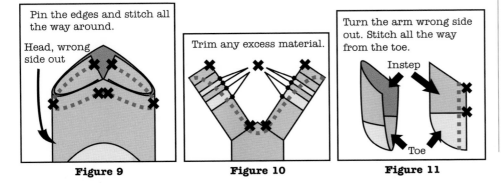

Figure 9   **Figure 10**   **Figure 11**

ESTELLE

Estelle might look simple to make, but she's uniquely prideful and will hold a long-standing grudge if you mess up her construction. So be mindful of the details.

> MY PATTERN'S WHOLESOME FUN FOR THE ENTIRE FAMILY. JUST TELL YOUR WIFE YOU'RE OUT BOWLING.

You Will Need

1 sock with a different colored heel (the color of the toe and any tube stripes won't matter)

The tube from a white or contrasting sock

A 1-1/2 x 3-inch (3.8 x 7.6 cm) rectangle of red or pink or tongue- colored sock material (like from that instep left over from the Red Wetty pattern!! Hint Hint)

Buttons for eyes

Blue or yellow fabric pencil or anything that can mark on fabric

Scissors

Needle and thread or sewing machine

Instructions

Cutting the Parts for Estelle

Arrange your colored sock with the heel facing up and the toe pointed DOWN this time (fig. 1).

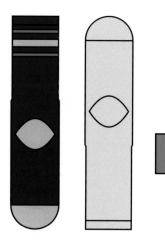

Figure 1

Cut a tall, tapering "bell curve" (get out your trigonometry books, or whatever-the-heck math that was) that peaks a little more than halfway between the heel and cuff. You can make the bell curve as tall as you want, really (figs. 2a and b).

Just below the heel and about ¹/₂ inch (1.3 cm) from either side, make two ³/₈-inch (9.5 mm) vertical cuts. These will be the slits for the arm attachments (fig. 2c).

About halfway between the heel and the toe, make a horizontal cut across the instep, severing it completely (fig. 2d).

Cut an almost square shape into the raw edge of the instep towards the heel. This serves as the "crotch," I guess. Make the square about one-third as wide as the width of the sock, and a little shorter than it is wide (fig. 2e).

Cut the toe from the part of the instep that you cut off right where the color changes, or right where the curve ends, whichever the case may be for your sock (fig. 2e).

Divide the resulting rectangle of instep in half diagonally. These triangles will be Estelle's arms (fig. 2f).

Whew. You got all that?

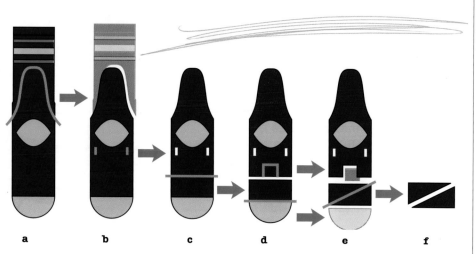

a   b   c   d   e   f

Figure 2

Arrange your bone-colored sock with the toe at the top and the heel facing up or down. It doesn't really matter how the heel is oriented.

Make two horizontal cuts removing the tube from the instep, and the cuff from the tube (fig. 3a).

Using a fabric pencil or some other marking implement that won't bleed all over the place, draw a thick bone shape on the tube. The bone shape should take up as much of the tube as it can, and the straight part of the bone, the part that con-nects the knobby shapes, should be preferably more, but no less than 1 inch (2.5 cm) wide (fig. 3b).

Cut out your bone shape, then cut the bone shape in half hor-izontally (fig. 3d).

You should now have four sep-arate pieces of half-bone shaped tube (fig. 3e).

You don't really need to do anything, as far as cutting, to your tongue fabric since it's already cut. If it isn't already cut, then find a tongue colored sock and cut out a 1-$\frac{1}{2}$ x 3 inch (4 to 8 cm) rectangle from the tube or the instep or wherever. Most of the time you can remove a horizontal bit of sock tube and cut along one of the folds. It's soooo easy.

Parts Overview (fig. 4)

After all that cutting and man-gling, you should have the fol-lowing parts for your Estelle creature:

1 stumpy-legged, peaky-headed body

2 triangles for arms

4 pieces that look like bones

1 strip of material for a tongue

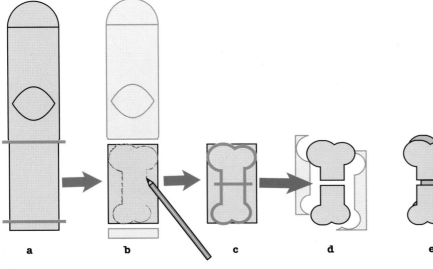

a   b   c   d   e

Figure 3

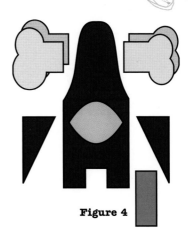

Figure 4

Stitching Estelle Together

STITCHING THE HEAD

Stitching Estelle together is pretty straightforward.

On the sides of the bell curve, stitch from the corners just above the heel to within 2 1/2 to 3 inches (6.4 to 7.6 cm) of the top of the curve (fig. 5b).

Then, start a new stitch across the top. Start about 1 inch (2.5 cm) above the end of the side stitch you just made. Continue across the top and stop about 1 inch (2.5 cm) above the end of the other side cut. Whatever you do, make the ends of the stitches match up reasonably (fig. 5a).

STITCHING THE FEET

Go down to the feet of the body sock. Make a downward-curving stitch starting from the folded edge of the foot. Continue across the bottom edge, curving upward to the horizontal crotch cut. Stop there. Don't seal up the crotch because you'll be stuffing through there. Do this again to the other foot (fig. 5c).

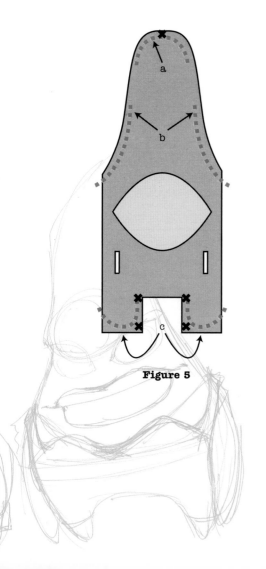

Figure 5

STITCHING THE ARMS

Grab one of the triangles made from a segment of tube. It should be folded at the narrowest/shortest end. Turn the piece so that the wrong side is out. Observe that the piece has a right angle.

Start stitching from the fold down the long side of the right angle towards the point. Turn upward at the point, and stitch up the other side, turning outward to the raw edge about ¹/₂ inch (1.3 cm) from the corner. You want to leave a little bit open for stuffing. Trim the excess material from the corner (fig. 6).

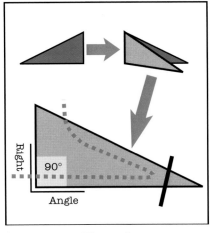

Figure 6

Turn the arm right side out. Stuff it firmly, leaving a good ¹/₄ to ¹/₂ inch (6 mm to 1.3 cm) unstuffed at the opening (fig. 7).

Repeat these instructions for the other arm.

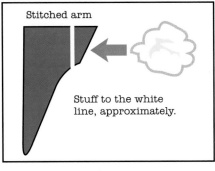

Stitched arm

Stuff to the white line, approximately.

Figure 7

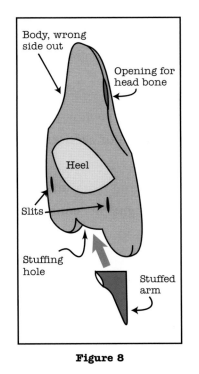

Body, wrong side out

Opening for head bone

Heel

Slits

Stuffing hole

Stuffed arm

Figure 8

This part's fun. Insert a stuffed arm up through the stuffing hole in the body (fig. 8).

Keep the long point down, and poke the arm's opening through one of the tiny slits below the heel. You might need to stretch the slit open a bit (fig. 9). Make the edges match up as best you can, and stitch the whole thing shut via the slit method (see page 24).

Repeat these instructions for the other arm.

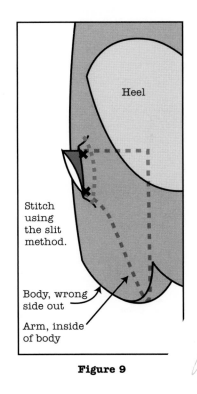

Heel

Stitch using the slit method.

Body, wrong side out

Arm, inside of body

Figure 9

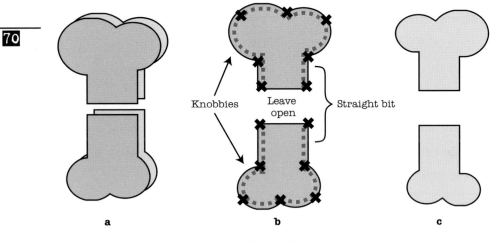

Figure 10

Turn the head bones right side out (fig. 10c).

Insert the head bones, knobbies first, into the holes you left in the sides of the head/bell curve (fig. 11). Match up the seams in the head bone with the seams in the head itself. It just looks better when seams match up as much as they can.

HEAD BONE

Now, friends, it is time for the head bone. This part is easy.

Take two matching halves, and face them, right side to right side (fig. 10a).

Place a pin at each corner and in the middle of each knobby to hold the whole lot in place. Start stitching from one corner of the straight bit, continuing around the knobbies, and back to the other corner of the straight bit (fig. 10b). Leave the ends of the straight bits open.

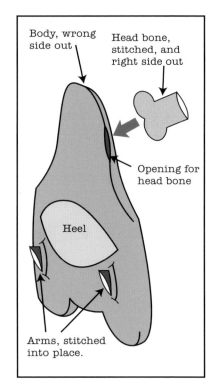

Figure 11

TONGUE

To make and attach the tongue, refer to the tongue-making instructions on page 29.

Congratulations! You're done stitching Estelle! Now just turn her right side out, stuff her firmly, and stitch her mouth (see page 26), and sew on her eyes.

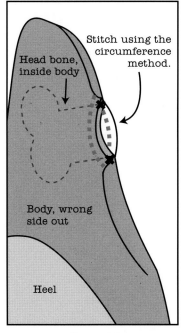

Stitch using the circumference method.

Head bone, inside body

Body, wrong side out

Heel

Figure 12

Pin the matching seams together. Stitch the head bone to the head using the circumference method (see page 23) (fig. 12).

Turn out the attached head bone to make room for the next one, and repeat these instructions.

SYD

Syd was one of the first stupid creatures, so he doesn't have what was to become the signature Stupid Creatures mouth. You only need one sock for Syd, which brings us to the very short materials list.

> SHOULD I TELL THEM HOW ATTRACTED TO ME THEY MIGHT BECOME IF THEY FOLLOW THIS PATTERN?

You Will Need

1 sock

Buttons for eyes

About 5 or 6 inches (13 or 15 cm) of the skinny part of a necktie

Scissors

Needle and thread or sewing machine

74

Cutting the Parts for Syd

Arrange your sock on its side so that its heel is pointing to the left or to the right, and the toe is decidedly angling to the other side. Make a horizontal cut halfway through the tube, removing the half with the cuff (fig. 1).

Cut this tube segment vertically in half. These segments will be the stubby little arms. From the cuff of each half, make a 1-inch (2.5 cm) (or so) cut directly in the middle. Make sure you cut through both layers of material. This cut will separate the thumb from the rest of the hand (fig. 2).

Keeping your sock arranged on its side, make a slit where the instep bends from ankle to foot, almost half the width of the sock. This will be Syd's mouth. Directly perpendicular to that slit, cut another slit about 3/4 inch (1.9 cm) long exactly in the middle of the sock. This slit and the end of the other one should be no less 1/2 inch (1.3 cm) apart. Go through both layers of the sock. This tiny cut will make the slits for Syd's arms (fig. 3).

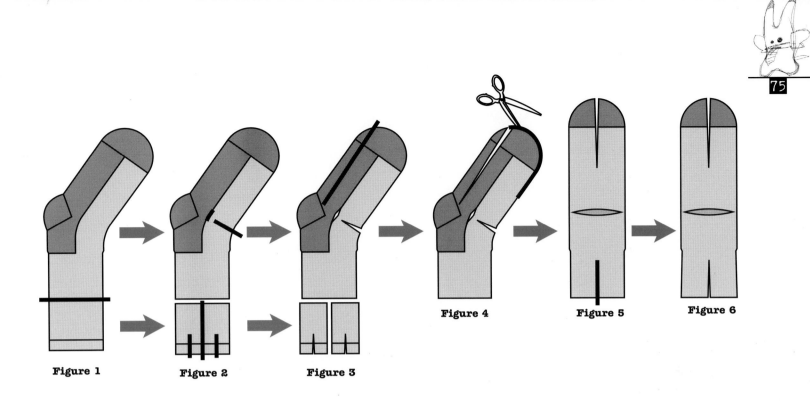

Figure 1

Figure 2

Figure 3

Figure 4

Figure 5

Figure 6

To make the cut for the tail, start from the toe. Cut from a point that's about 1 inch (2.5 cm) away from the edge of the sock. Continue cutting downward toward the heel, angling very gradually inward, and stopping level with the start of the heel (fig. 4).

Then, cut across the rounded top edge of the remaining wider part of the toe down to a point about half-way through the instep. Arrange your sock heel down. Make all the seams, corners, and edges match up right. Make a cut through the tube of the sock, smack in the middle, running vertically about 3 inches (7.6 cm) up toward the instep (fig. 5).

This cut will separate the legs (fig. 6).

Parts Overview (fig. 7)

Here's what your sock should look like when you're done cutting it.

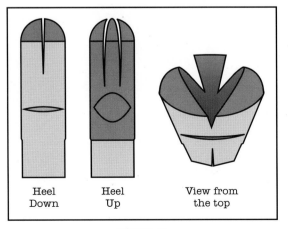

Heel Down

Heel Up

View from the top

Figure 7

Stitching Syd Together

This is gonna be fun, so put on some upbeat, happy music.

Turn the arm bits and the body piece wrong side out.

Stitch the raw edges shut in the arm bits, leaving as much seam allowance as you can 'cause I know they might be tiny (fig. 8).

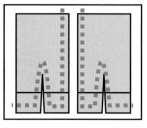

Figure 8

Stitch across the bottoms of the legs, then turn upward and stitch the leg cuts shut, stopping within $1/2$ inch (1.3 cm) of the vertex of that cut. This will be the stuff hole (fig. 9).

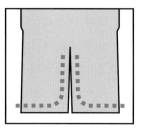

Figure 9

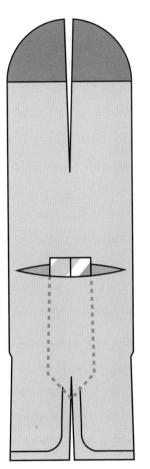

Figure 10

Keep the body piece with the mouth slit facing upwards and the heel facing down. Grab the despondent, lonely necktie piece and flip it over so you can see the folds and seams. Slide it into the mouth cut with its point (or finished edge, not the cut end) pointing downwards towards the legs (fig. 10).

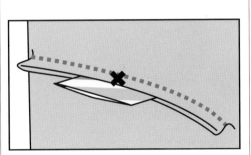

Figure 11

Figure 12

Close the mouth slit around the raw edge of the necktie. Pin the whole lot together right there in the middle. Stitch the mouth shut, sewing the necktie in place between the two layers. Essentially, use the slit method (see page 24) (fig. 11).

Turn the arm bits right side out and stuff them firmly, leaving a good ¼ to ½ inch (6 mm to 1.3 cm) of space unstuffed near the opening (fig. 12).

Insert the arm bits into the arm slits and pin them in place. Stitch it all shut using the slit method (see page 24) (fig. 13).

So far, so good.

Stop stuffing here.

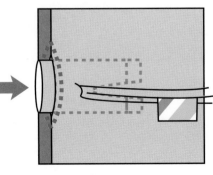

Figure 13

Next, turn the body piece to the side. Pin the raw edges of the tail together and stitch from the point of the tail all the way down and back up about halfway. Stop there (fig. 14).

Turn the body piece with the mouth slit facing up again. Pin the corner of the front ear cut to the point of the tail cut where you stopped stitching. Place a couple of pins along the remaining raw edges (fig. 15).

Start from the top of one ear and stitch the raw edges shut all the way down to the mid point at the base of the tail, and back up again to the point of the other ear (fig. 16).

There you go. You've stitched Syd. Turn him right side out again and stuff him firmly. Sew on buttons for eyes. Syd's mouth doesn't need to be completed like the other creatures' mouths, since there's no heel there.

This doesn't mean that in your own creature you can't transplant a heel into that spot (there are instructions for that on page 33) and put on a traditional mouth. It's your creature, so you make the rules.

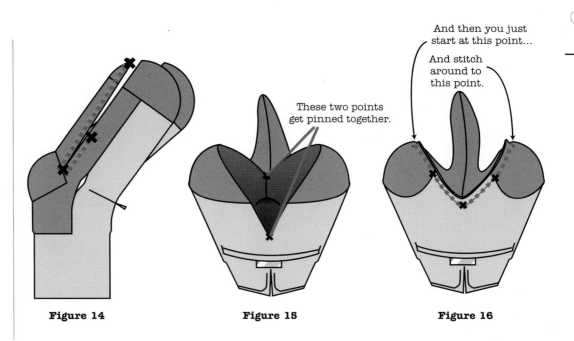

Figure 14

These two points get pinned together.

Figure 15

And then you just start at this point...

And stitch around to this point.

Figure 16

CLAUDE

Claude Grénache will never admit to loving a
certain domestic diva to the point of obsession,
but he will admit to his love for asparagus.
He auditioned for the part of Easter Bunny
during a college job fair, but was laughed away.

> MY PATTERN IS A CHALLENGE THAT FEW HAVE EVER ATTEMPTED.

You Will Need

2 socks, identical if possible,
but definitely similar in substance

Buttons for eyes

Scissors

Needle and thread or sewing machine

Cutting the Parts for Claude

Place both socks heel side up. Cut both socks vertically from the middle of the toe to about halfway between where the toe ends and the heel begins.

Coming in from the sides, about $3/4$ to 1 inch (1.9 to 2.5 cm) below the end of your first cut, cut at an angle, connecting with your first cut. Do this from both sides on both socks (fig. 1).

Pick one of your newly toeless socks to be the body. It doesn't matter which. They're equally disfigured at this point.

Make two cuts about $1\,1/4$ to $1\,1/2$ inches (3.1 to 3.8 cm) long starting from the cuff, each about one-quarter of the way in from the edge of the sock's tube. Make sure you cut

through both layers of sock material (so that you get four cuts in total) (fig. 2).

Follow the tail variation of the neck-making instructions on page 30 (fig. 3a).

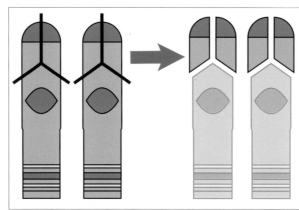

Figure 1   **Figure 2**

Parts Overview (fig. 5)

If you've done everything correctly you should have the following parts for assembly into your Claude creature:

1 badly mutilated majority of a sock that you'll use for the head and body

2 squares of cuff material for the ears

4 bits of toe that will become the legs

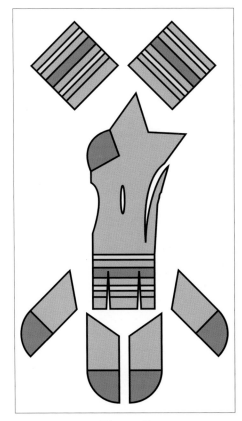

You'll have already done your neck cuts (fig. 3b).

Grab the sock from which you cut leg parts. Cut horizontally about halfway through the tube. Reserve the half with the cuff for the ears. Keep the remainder of the sock for another project (fig. 4a).

Next, cut the tube segment in half vertically (fig. 4b).

Unfold each half of the tube segment so that you have two squares or rectangles or whatever the case may be (fig. 4c).

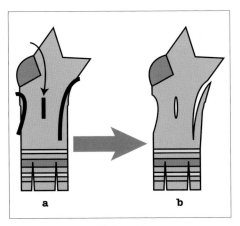

Figure 3

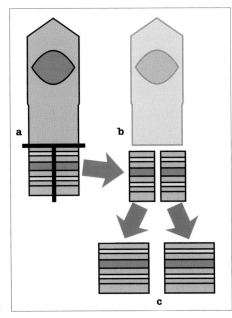

Figure 4

Figure 5

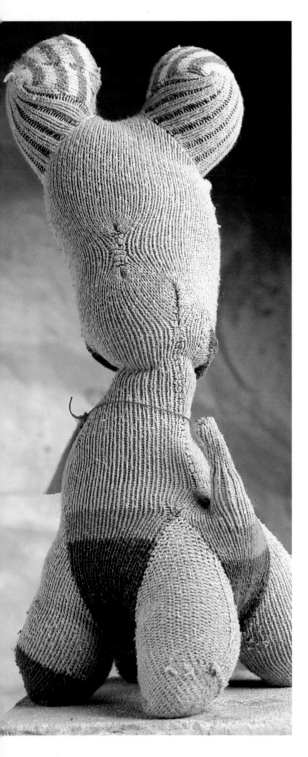

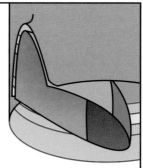
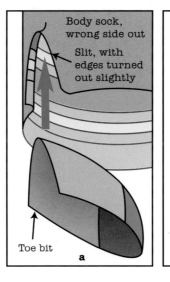

Body sock, wrong side out

Slit, with edges turned out slightly

Toe bit

a

Match up the edges as closely as you can.

b

c

Figure 6

Stitching Claude Together

Everybody get comfortable. This one will take some patience. Let's start with the body. Turn it wrong side out.

STITCHING THE NECK AND TAIL

Follow the tail variation of the neck-making instructions on page 30.

STITCHING THE LEGS TO THE BODY, PART 1

So, you've got a toe bit and the body sock with the neck and tail sewn.

Arrange the toe bit as so, beneath one of the slits in the cuff of the body sock (fig. 6a). The edge of the toe bit ought to match up with the size of the slit, but it really doesn't matter unless the toe bit's edge is much bigger than the slit. In this instance, cut the slit a little deeper in the body sock to compensate (figs. 6a and 6b).

Arrange the edge of the toe bit inside the slit of the body sock with right sides touching. The vertex of the slit should match up with the edge of the toe bit at its fold. The corners of the slit and the toe bit should correspond (fig. 6c).

Pin the two pieces together at the corresponding corners and at the meeting of the toe bit's fold and the slit's vertex.

Stitch the two edges together as you see in fig. 6c. Remember the seam allowance of ¼ inch (6 mm). Turn the toe bit out so that it hangs from the outside of the body.

Repeat these steps with the remaining toe bits. Once you've done one, the rest should be a snap.

STITCHING THE LEGS TO THE BODY, PART TWO

Okay, please try to be respectful as we stare plainly up Claude's chute. This view is essential to the next step. The places you should pin on the leg are as follows: a) where the color changes from toe to instep b) the edges of the seam from body to leg, and c) about one-third of the way into the body from the edge of the leg. At the end of it all, you'll be left with a hole

for turning and stuffing. Bear in mind that everything's still wrong side out in this diagram (fig. 7).

STITCHING THE EARS

Grab one of the squares of tube you made for the ears. Arrange it right side up like this (fig. 8a).

Fold the top edge down to meet the bottom edge (fig. 8b).

Pin the edges together near the corners and stitch from edge to fold leaving ¼-inch (6 mm) seam allowance (fig. 8c).

Turn the ear so that the newly made seams face you (fig. 8d).

Pin the seams together at the edges where they meet, and stitch from a side fold, just over the seam, and then immediately down to the open edge (fig. 8e).

Then turn it right side out and BING, you have an ear. Repeat these instructions with the other ear (fig. 8f).

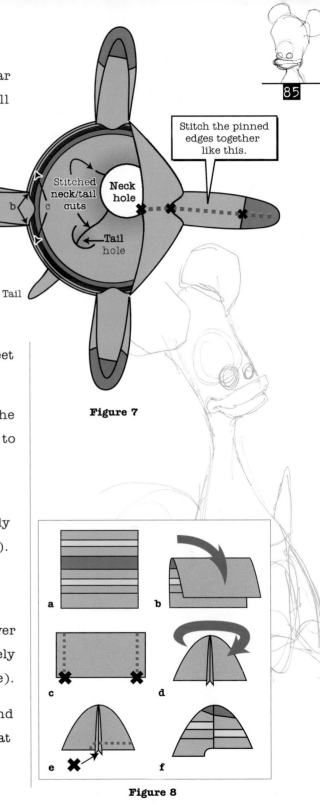

Stitch the pinned edges together like this.

Figure 7

Figure 8

Stitching the Ears to the Head

Grab the body sock, keep it right side out. You remember that peak leftover where the toe bits were removed? It's now the top of the head (fig. 9a). Place a pin at the top corners of both layers of material.

Make a stitch across the head opening, leaving one-quarter of

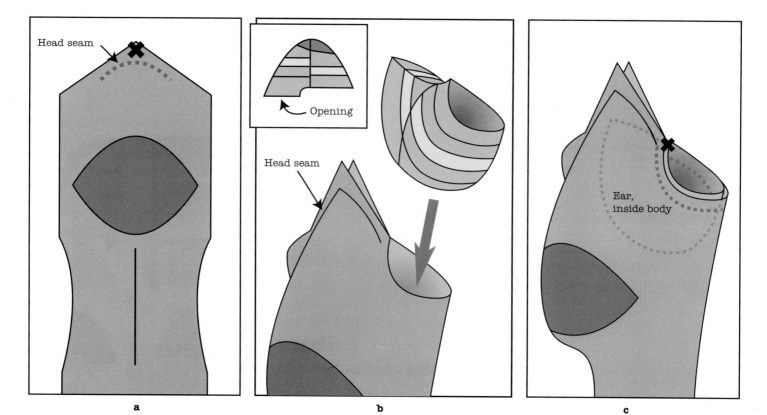

Head seam

Opening

Head seam

Ear, inside body

a   b   c

Figure 9

the opening on either edge unstitched and open. Okay. Now that those instructions for the ear are all taken care of, you have a little ear. Orient it so that the opening is up (fig. 9b).

You've made your stitch at the top of the head, which left you with two openings for the ears to slip down into. Insert the ear into either of these holes. Match up the seam of the ear with the point where the head seam ends (fig. 9c). Pin those seam points together, and stitch the ear edge to the head opening edge using the circumference method. Repeat these instructions for the other ear.

Your Claude creature is now assembled. Gently turn him right side out, taking care not to pop any of the stitches you've made. Use your point turner for the tail and ears if you need it. Now you're ready to stuff, sew shut, and finish

your quadruped with a mouth and a pair of eyes. This is truly a momentous occasion and if you're of age, you should pop open some champagne. If

you're not of age make a big, gooey s'more in the toaster oven (without the tray!).

GENEVIEVE

Genevieve is definitely for the skilled stupid creature maker, but I think that with a little concentration, anyone can make her. I mean, I just eyeballed the whole thing the first time I made her. There really is no science to any of this.

PUBLIC NOTICE:

THE IMPLEMENTATION OF THIS PATTERN AND SET OF INSTRUCTIONS COULD RESULT IN A 17% INCREASE IN CORPORATE EVIL ON A GALACTIC SCALE. RESPONSIBILITY BEFALLS THE INDIVIDUAL CRAFTSPERSON.

You Will Need

2 socks, identical if possible, but definitely similar in substance

1 sock of a contrasting color or pattern

Buttons for eyes

Scissors

Needle and thread or sewing machine

Cutting the Pieces for Genevieve

Arrange one of your matched socks heel up with the toe at

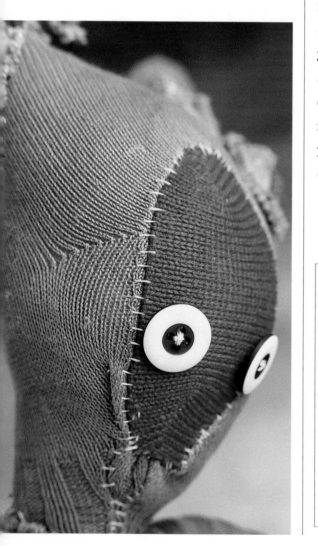

the top. Remove a 1-inch (2.5 cm) wide strip from the toe and instep, stopping about 1 1/2 inches (3.8 cm) above the heel. Remove the heel and keep it for another creature. Remove or extend the cuff because you're going to do a lot of sewing down there and you don't want bunched up extra material making it hard to pierce your needle through (figs. 1a and 1b).

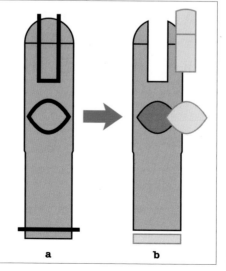

Figure 1

Continue to disfigure this sock by following the neck-making instructions on page 30. Genevieve doesn't get a tail.

At the cuff, make two 3/4-inch (1.9 cm) cuts through both layers of fabric, about one-quarter of the distance in from either edge of the sock. These are notches for the feet (fig. 2).

Figure 2

Grab the other sock from the matched pair. Cut off the toe and keep it for another monster. Make a horizontal cut below the cut that severed the toe so that the resulting segment is as close to being a perfect square as possible without cutting into the heel (figs. 3a, b, and c).

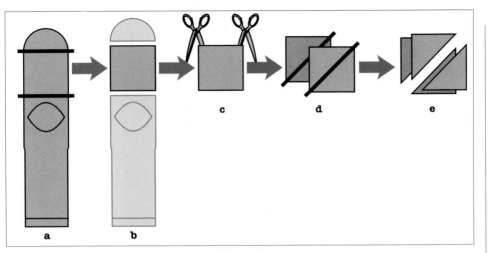

Figure 3

Cut that square segment along both edges so that two single-layer squares result (fig. 3d).

Finally, cut these two squares diagonally, resulting in four wide triangles (fig. 3e).

Remove the cuff from the tube of the same sock that provided Genny's feet. Cut four segments each about 1 inch (2.5 cm) wide, no more than 1 1/2 inches (3.8 cm) from the tube. You might use up all of your tube, you might not. Keep any excess sock for another project. The point isn't to divide the tube equally into fourths, but to cut 4-inch (10 cm)-or-so-wide segments from your tube (figs. 4a and 4b).

If your sock isn't long enough to make 4-inch (10 cm) -or-so-wide segments, use the tube of a long enough sock (but not the sock you're using for this creature's body), or cut your tube into whatever width will result in an even four. I know this sounds picky, but don't go below 3/4 inch (1.9 cm).

Cut your 4-inch (10 cm) or-so-wide segments along one folded edge, keeping the other edge intact (fig. 4c).

Figure 4d only exists to show the nature of the four resulting strips of fabric you should have.

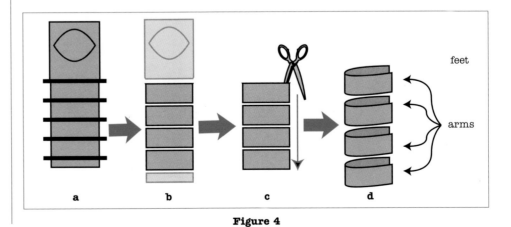

Figure 4

Take the third sock (the matchless one) and remove the toe and cuff. Keep the toe for another monster. Discard the cuff unless you really want to keep it (fig. 5a).

Cut out the heel, allowing at least a ¼-inch (6 mm) border around it. If your sock is solid colored, just guestimate this measurement. This disembodied heel will be the faceplate for your Genevieve (figs. 5a and 5b).

The sock is completely bereft of any substantial or useful qualities. It might make a decent dusting rag or something to pin upon the wall and hate.

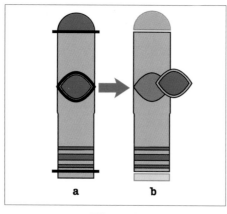

Figure 5

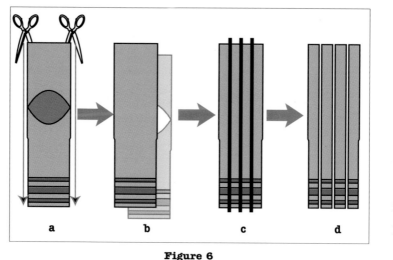

Figure 6

But we've got plans to desecrate it further. Cut this disemboweled sock from instep to tube down both edges. Discard

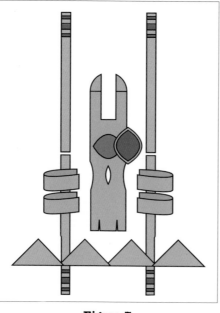

Figure 7

the layer where the heel used to be, or keep it for another monster. Cut the remaining layer into four equal lengthwise strips from instep to tube. These will be the ribbons for your Genevieve (figs. 6a, 6b, 6c, and 6d).

Parts Overview (fig. 7)

Genny has a lot of pieces. Hopefully they aren't too many or too confusing. You should have:

1 badly-tormented piece of heelless sock for the head and body

4 arm bits

4 triangles for the feet

1 disembodied heel for the face plate

4 long strips of sock for ribbons

Stitching Genevieve Together

Take a deep breath, walk around the block once or twice, get some sunshine on your face. This might take a while. Of course, you might be smarter and faster than me, which is likely. But really, don't stress. The best way to tackle a complicated set of tasks is just to calmly do one thing at a time. But keep some tissues and chocolates on hand for sobbing into and restoring your cheer.

One thing I'll go ahead and tell you is different about Genny is that her arms are attached to her outside once she's stuffed. If you don't want to do it that way, I recommend using the slit method (see page 24) for attaching her limbs because so much is going on with her body already.

You know what I mean? You might not have enough room for four armholes.

STITCHING THE FACE AND BODY

Here's the weird part. You're gonna have to manipulate the hole a little to accommodate the disembodied heel. Grafting the heel on at a 90° angle to the orientation of the hole will achieve that vertical almond/diamond look for Genevieve's face. Use the circumference method (see page 23) to attach the heel to the

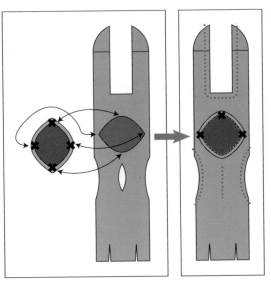

Figure 8   **Figure 9**

hole, and BING, you've got a face for your Genevieve (figs. 8 and 9).

Next stitch shut the neck cuts as explained in the neck-making instructions on page 30. Stitch shut the raw edges between Genevieve's ear thingies (fig. 9).

YAY, the body for Genevieve is done. Onward to the arms and feet.

STITCHING THE ARMS

The arms are easy. In fact, they're so easy it's almost a travesty to have their instructions in a how-to book. There ought to be a new genre of book called a "well-duh" book, in which these arm instructions would appear next to "how to have fingers."

Fold the arm strip in half vertically, with right sides touching (fig. 10a).

Stitch down one long edge, going across the fold in a U pattern, and come back up the other long edge (fig. 10b).

Don't forget the seam allowance. How much should you leave? It's right there in the "well-duh" book next to the entry about the color of the sky. Do this for all four arms and turn them right side out (fig. 10c).

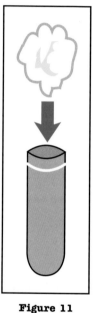

Take the arms you've just stitched and stuff them to a uniform firmness. Leave yourself $1/4$-inch (6 mm) of unstuffed space at the opening of each arm (fig. 11).

Figure 11

STITCHING THE FEET

Arrange one of the triangles you've cut for the feet right side up with the widest segment at the top, and the opposing point down (fig. 12a).

Fold the left corner over to meet the right corner (fig. 12b).

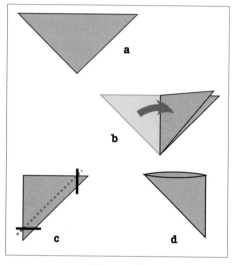

Figure 12

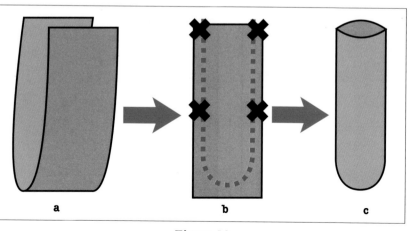

Figure 10

Stitch the two edges together. Leave what seam allowance you can, 'cause the pieces might be kind of small. If you have enough material for a $^1/_4$ inch (6 mm), go for it. If you don't, do the best you can or do an overcast or zigzag stitch.

Trim the corners off the seam allowance to ease turning and stuffing.

Turn the foot right side out. Repeat these instructions for the other three feet (fig. 12d).

Attaching the Feet to the Body

To attach the feet to the body, use the circumference method (see page 23).

Turn the body wrong side out. Take a finished foot and pin the seam to the open edges of one of the four cuts at the bottom of the body, right sides touching. The point of the foot should be inside the body. Pin the edge of the foot opening directly opposite the seam to the corner of the leg cut (fig. 13a).

Stitch the edges together leaving a $^1/_4$-inch (6 mm) seam allowance (fig. 13b).

Repeat these instructions for the other three feet. Once the feet are attached to the body, turn everything right side out.

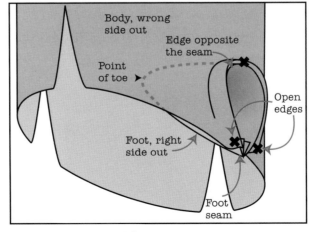

Figure 13a

Body, wrong side out
Edge opposite the seam
Point of toe ▶
Open edges
Foot, right side out
Foot seam

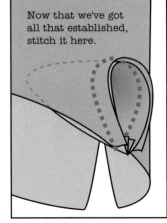

Figure 13b

Now that we've got all that established, stitch it here.

Stuffing and Closing the Body

Stuff the body firmly (fig. 14).

Once the body is stuffed, close up the bottom. Here's how you do that:

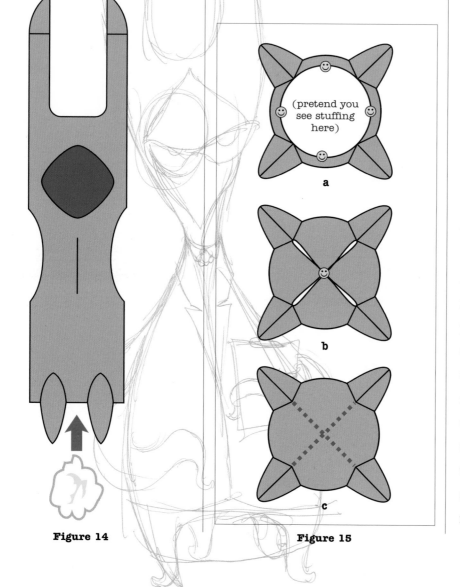

Figure 14

Arrange your finished body with the opening and the bottoms of the feet facing upward so that you're staring directly at Genny's bits and pieces. Imagine little smiley faces exactly in the midpoint between each foot (fig. 15a).

(pretend you see stuffing here)

a

b

c

Figure 15

Converge all the smiley faces into the center of the stuff hole and lock them all together with a few overcast stitches. You should have kind of an X where the stuffing is still exposed (fig. 15b).

Stitch the segments of the X shut with a ladder or overcast stitch (see page 19) (fig. 15c).

There you go! She's closed up!

Attaching the Arms

Take two of the four stuffed arms. Align their open ends and pin them to Genny's body where you think her shoulders should go. You can do this many different ways. I recommend the overcast stitch (see page 19) to attach the arms. Secure your thread on Genevieve's body, and just go for it. Overcast the dickens out of the tops of the arms. Get them onto the body so firmly that the thread builds up into a glob. You can't sew these on firmly enough (fig. 16).

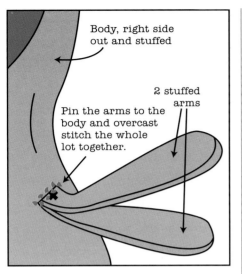

Body, right side out and stuffed

2 stuffed arms

Pin the arms to the body and overcast stitch the whole lot together.

Figure 16

Take the other two arms and repeat the overcasting process on the other side of the body, or wherever you want two more arms to go.

If you want, you can stitch the arms to the body individually. It's all up to you.

RIBBONS

You've got four strips of sock tube and instep. Starting with two of them, with wrong sides facing up, bump like ends together. Use an overcast stitch to attach the two strips to each other. Use the overcast stitch, or a wide zigzag stitch on the raw edges of the ribbon to keep the edges from fraying (fig. 17).

There. Now you've made a ribbon. Repeat these instructions for the other two strips.

Tie the ribbons you've made in bows around Genny's ear thingies. Sew buttons onto the face patch for eyes. Use as many as you'd like. Genevieve doesn't get a mouth like the other creatures.

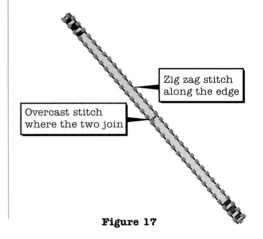

Zig zag stitch along the edge

Overcast stitch where the two join

Figure 17

Look at All the Spare Parts

You Have Left Over!

The neatest thing about this craft is that often the remnants are useful. Here are some suggestions for how to use the parts that didn't become sock monsters. The more you mix and match, the better, often, the monster becomes. Bear in mind that you can't make all these suggested monsters with these parts. For example, Part N is used quite a bit because it has so much potential. You get to decide how your Part N is best used.

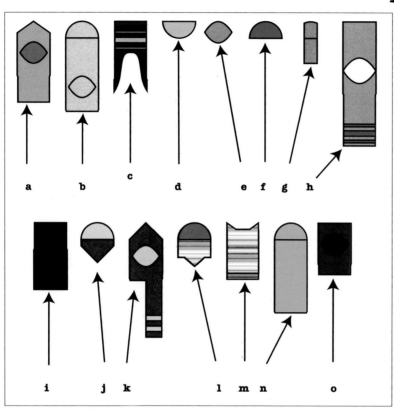

a   b   c   d   e   f   g   h

i   j   k   l   m   n   o

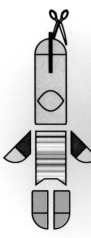

Head and Ears: Part B, with a cut through the toe and part of the instep

Arms: Part J, cut in half vertically

Body: Part M

Legs: The toe half of Part N

Idea #1

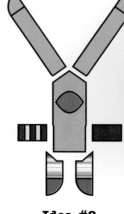

Ears: Part N, cut in half vertically

Head and Body: Part A

Arms: That half-tube hanging off of Part K, cut in half horizontally

Legs: Part L, cut in half vertically

Idea #2

Horns: Part F, cut vertically in half

Head: Part K with that half-strip of tube removed

Tail: The half-strip of tube from Part K

Arms: Part J, cut in half vertically

Body and Legs: Part N, with a cut through the toe and part of the instep

Idea #3

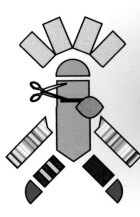

Head and Body: Part A, heel-side down, and with a slit cut for transplanting a mouth

Mouth: Part E

Top of Head: The toe from Part N

Head Thingies: Part B, with the toe removed and cut into horizontal quarters

Arms: Part M, cut vertically in half

Legs: The strip of half-tube from Part K, cut in half horizontally

Feet: Part F, cut in half vertically

Idea #5

Ears: Part C

Head: Part O

Mouth: Part E

Arms: Part N

Body and Legs: Part B, with a cut through the toe and part of the instep

Tail: Part G

Idea #4

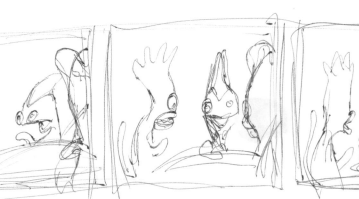

Gallery

THE CUSTOMER WHO ORDERED HER, A DEDICATED "CREATURE OF HABIT," ORDERED 14 CREATURES IN TOTAL.
Photo by John Murphy

I STUFFED HIM IN A CAFÉ BACK IN OAKLAND. MY FRIEND GRETCHEN WALKED IN AND TOLD ME HE LOOKED LIKE A DUNCAN. THE NAME STUCK, AND NOW HE'S ONE OF THE MOST SOUGHT-AFTER CREATURE BODY TYPES IN THE COLLECTION.
Photo by John Murphy

AMIT
HERE'S A CREATURE MADE ENTIRELY OF REMNANTS AND SCRAP MATERIAL. HE SOLD IN A HEARTBEAT AND I SORT OF REGRET LETTING HIM GO.
Photo by John Murphy

GRUGWICK IS NEW ROCHELLE'S SIX-Y... RECORD HOLDER FOR BREATH HOLDING... HAS YET TO EXHALE FROM THE FIRST O... HE ENTERED. THAT'S WHY HIS EYES HA... POPPED OUT TO THE SIDES. THE OXYGE... RIVATION DID FUNNY THINGS TO THE P... SURE IN HIS HEAD.

FREAKSHOW

THIS GUY WAS THE BIGGEST OF FIVE ORDERED TO COMMEMORATE THE BIRTH OF THE CUSTOMER'S SON. HE CAME UP WITH ALL THE NAMES.
Photo by John Murphy

WITH A GANG OF LOCAL SOCK MONKEYS SINCE ARRIVING AT HIS NEW HOME IN SAN MATEO, CALIFORNIA.
From the Collection of Amy and Ernie Prows

DON'T BE FOOLED BY **JOANIE**'S CALM EXTERIOR. SHE MAY LOOK LIKE A MILD MANNERED SECRETARY ON THE OUTSIDE, BUT SHE'S REALLY A MUNICIPAL SANITATION COMMISSIONER.
Photo by John Murphy

LEEM AND HER SIBLINGS (NOT SHOWN) WERE ALL MADE FROM ONE LITTLE PAIR OF HEART-MOTIF SOCKS THAT MEANT A LOT TO THEIR OWNER STEPHANIE ALDRIDSON.
From the Collection of Stephanie Aldridson

BRAVELIVER

WHEN EMILY RUSSO ORDERED A TRADITIONAL SCOTTISH "GREAT KILT," FOR HER CREATURE, I JUMPED AT THE CHALLENGE. BRAVELIVER RESIDES IN SCOTLAND NOW. ISN'T THAT THE GREATEST?!

THIS IS **BOX HEAD**. HE WON'T SAY WHAT HIS REAL NAME IS, BUT WE THINK HE'S UGLY.

MIGHTY KLIMZON WELL LOVED BY THE NEW YORK CITY GRAPHIC DESIGNER WITH WHOM HE LIVES. IN FACT, UPON HIS ARRIVAL AT HIS NEW HOME, KLIMZON SENT ME A POST CARD. IT WAS SWEET.

LARZ LIVES IN SOMERVILLE, MASSACHUSSETS, WHERE EVERYONE PRONOUNCES HIS NAME "LAAAHS."

HELLO, MY NAME IS
LARZ

GLELNA POSES DUTIFULLY, MODELING A STYLISH HEAD

THIS IS **BOYD**, THE
ONLY STUPID CREATURE
FOR WHOM A MUSTACHE
WAS REQUESTED.
Photo by John Murphy

GORDON POSES INTRO-
SPECTIVELY OVER THE
OAKLAND SKYLINE.
Photo by John Murphy

ICHABOD POSES IN RED
TULLE (HE LOST A BET
AND HAD TO WEAR IT TO
THE GROCERY STORE).
Photo by John Murphy

SZLAPPA'S OWNER
BRIAN DORE SAYS
"EVERYONE WOULD
BE HAPPIER WITH A
STUPID CREATURE
IN THEIR LIVES."
**From the Collection
of Brian Dore**

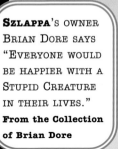

HELLO, MY NAME IS.
SZLAPPA

PERCY AND BYSSHE
THESE GUYS WERE NAMED FOR PERCY BYSSHE SHELLY, THE
HUSBAND OF FRANKENSTEIN AUTHOR MARY
WALSTONCRAFT SHELLEY. I FIGURED MARY MUST HAVE DONE
SOME EMPIRICAL RESEARCH FOR THE GRUESOME TALE. THIS
DUAL CREATURE IS MY HOMAGE TO THE FATE WHICH VERY
LIKELY BEFELL HER HUSBAND.

Gallery

TOASTY'S HUMBLE BEGINNINGS AS A TOASTER COVER HAVE NOT STOPPED HIM FROM BECOMING A PRODIGIOUS WORLD TRAVELER. HE NOW LIVES IN HONG KONG.
From the collection of Carrie Wallace Brown. Photo courtesy of Carrie Wallace Brown

SUSAN GOT A CAMEO IN MY STUPID COMIC SERIES (AT WWW.STUPIDCREATURES.COM) AS ESTELLE'S DUNDERING SIDEKICK. I HOPE TO BRING HER BACK AS A REGULAR CHARACTER AS TIME GOES ON.
Photo by John Murphy

GUWELDA WAS NAMED FOR A FRIEND OF MY FORMER ROOMMATE. I JUST COULDN'T LET THE NAME SLIP AWAY. NOT SURE IF I SPELLED IT RIGHT THOUGH.
Photo by John Murphy

ARPHAXADDA IS GOING TO SAN FRANCISCO. SHE'S ONE OF MY MORE INTERESTING DESIGNS.

A NICE PORTRAIT OF **HLAB**.
Photo by John Murphy

HELLO, MY NAME IS
(TOASTY)

HIM 1 AND **HIM 2**, ANGEL AND DEVIL TWINS. THESE WERE A SERIOUSLY FUN PAIR TO MAKE.
Photo by John Murphy

HOOPER SUEMAN IS THE ONLY STUPID CREATURE WHO CAN FLY. HE DOES IT OFTEN TO SHOW OFF HOW COOL HE IS.
From the collection of Danielle Jarred.
Photo by Danielle Jarred

MR. FERGUS HAS KEPT THRONGS AND THRONGS OF HAPPY SENIOR CITIZENS ENTERTAINED FOR MOST OF HIS LIFE. **From the Collection of Terry Taylor**

MUNTHA SUNDAYS AND **CAMI** GOOF AROUND ON A BEAUTIFUL AFTERNOON.
Photo by John Murphy

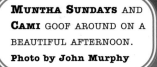

GRUPHUDD EUBANCHS IS GOING TO NEW YORK TO LIVE WITH REPEAT CUSTOMER LISA GELLER, A PROOFREADER AND TOY COLLECTOR. **From the collection of Lisa Geller**

Gallery

BANDIT WAS MADE FROM SOCKS MY PAL RORI GAVE ME. I'M KEEPING BANDIT FOR MYSELF.

BERTL NOVACK POSES AGAINST A TREE-LINED MORNING SKY. **Photo by John Murphy**

GOOD OLD **DORIS**. SHE MAKES A LOUSY QUICHE EVEN AFTER MONTHS OF HYPNOTHERAPY. **Photo by John Murphy**

BLANGLES MADE A LOUSY JESTER, TO BE HONEST. ALL HE EVER WANTED TO DO WAS RUN A SUBWAY TRAIN IN SOME BIG CITY. BUT ALAS, WE MUST DO THE WORK WE'VE BEEN GIVEN TO DO. **Photo by John Murphy**

SERAPHINA ALSO HAS A TINY CAMEO IN ESTELLE'S SCENES IN THE COMIC (AT WWW.STUPIDCREATURES.COM) FOR DESIGN REASONS, THOUGH, I CHANGED HER COLORATION SOME. SHE'S NOW GREEN WITH YELLOW LIPS. AH WELL. **Photo by John Murphy**

NIANG ALSO WENT TO PARAMOUNT STUDIOS WITH LAUREL. WOULDN'T IT BE FUNNY IF HE WOUND UP AS A PROP?
Photo by John Murphy

ARLINGTON FISHBAUGH STANDS WITLESSLY IN FRONT OF A WITHERED, DEAD PLANT NEAR A BUNCH OF CONDOS.
Photo by John Murphy

MR. BUNNY THE FISHFACED GORILLA DOG WAS PROBABLY THE THIRD STUPID CREATURE EVER MADE. THEY WEREN'T EVEN CALLED STUPID CREATURES AT THE TIME. HE RESIDES IN ASHEVILLE WITH A 2-YEAR-OLD NAMED TOBY.

QUEEP PROBABLY THE MOST LIKED OF THE "SCHIFINO EIGHT," THIS ONE WAS KEPT AS THE CUSTOMER'S OWN AFTER THE OTHER SEVEN WERE DISBURSED.
Photo by John Murphy

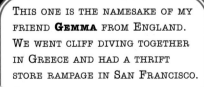

THIS ONE IS THE NAMESAKE OF MY FRIEND **GEMMA** FROM ENGLAND. WE WENT CLIFF DIVING TOGETHER IN GREECE AND HAD A THRIFT STORE RAMPAGE IN SAN FRANCISCO.

Gallery

HANS ENJOYS HAVING FANGS. EVER SINCE HE GOT THEM HE'S HAD NO TROUBLE EATING THINGS LIVE.

MR. CRUMPLESANDWICH IS MOVING TO ASTORIA SOON. HE HOPES TO SEE SOME BIRDS.

FRIEDA WISHES SHE WERE MORE COLORFUL.

IF **SQUASHPASTE** HOLDS HIS HEAD JUST SO, HE CAN TUNE INTO PRO BASEBALL BROADCASTS WITH HIS RECEPTOR HEAD WANDS.

MASSACHUSETTS COLLEGE OF ART STUDENT LIZ ASHWORTH LOVED HER "SOCKTOPUS" **WILLOUGBY** SO MUCH SHE BASED HER THESIS PROJECT ON HIM.

Photos courtesy of Liz Ashworth

Gallery

DESPERADO NOW LIVES IN BROOKLYN WITH HIS FRIEND JENNY, A FILM AFFICIONADO.

DAVINA CAME FROM A LONG LINE OF CIRCUS PERFORMERS WHO ESCAPED FROM CRUEL RINGMASTERS.

BONESQUISHER IS A SURVIVOR OF AN INTERSTELLAR DROP FROM EARTH. ALL THAT WAS INJURED WAS A BIT OF HIS LOWER LEFT RIB.

THWIP CAN WALK MUCH FASTER USING HIS ARMS, SO HE OFTEN DOES.

CHRISTOPHE LOVES HAVING FOUR ARMS, THOUGH HIS UPPER TWO DON'T SEEM TO BE ABLE TO POINT DOWNWARD.

COARSEAPPLE IS RATHER FOND OF SARDINE TINS. SHE COLLECTS THEM FOR AIR FRESHENERS IN HER CEDAR CLOSETS.

SARGG WAS NAMED FOR HIS THROATY GROWL. IF YOU HEAR IT, RUN. IT MEANS HE'S ABOUT TO BITE YOU.

THIS IS **PIXEL**. WHEN SHE ISN'T LENDING HER ARMS OUT AS DOUBLE DUTCH JUMPING ROPES, SHE TEACHES PILATES.

Index

About the Author

John Murphy double majored in illustration and ceramics at East Carolina University in Greenville, North Carolina, where he also wrote comics for the student-run newspaper and served as the comics page editor. This experience helped Murphy land the position as Newsroom Artist at **Wilmington** (North Carolina) **Star News**. When he wasn't designing or illustrating freelance, Murphy continued to pursue ceramic sculpture, winding up as the first-ever male member of Berkeley, California's Mudwomen ceramic studio. After a layoff in 2003, Murphy turned to sewing socks into monsters. What started as a casual pursuit became a career in less than a year, as the "Stupid Creatures" gained national and international attention.